CLINICAL COUNSELLING IN PASTORAL SETTINGS

A substantial amount of counselling is conducted by people who either work in religious settings or whose work is influenced by their religious belief. There are, however, few books available which help such counsellors with the practical issues raised by working with this religious dimension.

Clinical Counselling in Pastoral Settings highlights the cultural, spiritual and professional aspects of counselling in pastoral settings, exploring key issues such as the significance of religious tradition in this setting, appropriate professional boundaries, and the nature of transference and countertransference. Other chapters discuss how counsellors can respond therapeutically to those who have experienced abuse in religious settings and the challenges that are associated with pastoral counselling work.

Combining theoretical discussions with relevant case material, *Clinical Counselling in Pastoral Settings* will be a useful resource for anyone involved in therapeutic work which has a religious dimension, as well as those training to become pastoral counsellors or carers.

Gordon Lynch lectures in counselling at University College Chester, and is a qualified and practising counsellor.

Contributors: David Lyall; Emmanuel Lartey; Alistair Ross; Jessica Rose; Alan Boyd; Barrie Hinksman; Ruth Layzell; John Foskett.

CLINICAL COUNSELLING IN CONTEXT
Series Editor: John Lees

This series of key texts examines the unique nature of counselling in a wide range of clinical settings. Each book shows how the context in which counselling takes place has profound effects on the nature and outcome of the counselling practice, and encourages clinical debate and dialogue.

CLINICAL COUNSELLING IN PASTORAL SETTINGS

Edited by Gordon Lynch

London and New York

First published 1999 by Routledge
11 New Fetter Lane, London EC4P 4EE

Simultaneously published in the USA and Canada
by Routledge
29 West 35th Street, New York, NY 10001

Typeset in Times by Keystroke, Jacaranda Lodge, Wolverhampton
Printed and bound in Great Britain by MPG Books Ltd, Bodmin

British Library Cataloguing in Publication Data
A catalogue record for this book is available from the British Library

Library of Congress Cataloguing in Publication Data
Clinical counselling in pastoral settings / edited by Gordon Lynch.
p. cm. (Clinical counselling in context series)
Includes bibliographical references and index.
1. Pastoral counseling. I. Lynch, Gordon, 1968– . II. Series.
BV4012.2.C536 1999
253.5 – dc21
99–18232
CIP

ISBN 0–415–19675–2 (hbk)
ISBN 0–415–19676–0 (pbk)

CONTENTS

CONTRIBUTORS

Alan Boyd has been a whole-time chaplain at the Birmingham Heartlands and Solihull Hospital Trust for the last ten years. His interest in counselling was first kindled at theological college and he has continued to integrate it into his ministry firstly in the parish, then as a university chaplain and now as a hospital chaplain. He is presently studying for an MA in Psychodynamic Counselling at the University of Birmingham.

John Foskett is an Anglican priest and was chaplain to the Bethlem and Maudsley NHS Trust as well as being a parish priest. He has been involved in the practice of pastoral care and counselling for all of his ministry, was a founder and is an active member of the Association for Pastoral Care and Counselling and the British Association for Counselling of which he is a Fellow. He has been involved in both the European and international pastoral care and counselling movements. He writes and lectures on pastoral counselling, supervision, and religion and mental health.

Barrie Hinksman has, until recently, practised counselling and psychotherapy. He has taught those subjects in a number of contexts. He is completing a research project at the University of Birmingham on gender in Gestalt therapy and feminist theology. He is a member of the congregation at Coventry Cathedral.

Emmanuel Lartey is Senior Lecturer in Pastoral Studies in the Department of Theology at Birmingham University. He is an ordained Methodist minister, and before coming to Birmingham lectured in Practical Theology at the University of Ghana, Legon. He is a member of the Executive Committee of both the International Council for Pastoral Care and Counselling and the International Academy of Practical Theology, as well as being the current Chair of the British and Irish Association for Practical Theology. He has a particular interest in inter-cultural approaches to pastoral care and counselling, which he explored in his recent book, *In Living Colour*, and is the editor of a new journal, *Black Theology in Britain*.

Ruth Layzell studied for a degree in Modern Languages at Oxford University, and then subsequently undertook postgraduate studies at Nottingham University to train as a social worker. After qualifying, she worked for ten years in the field, initially in a generic team and later as a specialist child care and family placement worker. She joined the staff at St John's College, Nottingham in 1991 to take up a post as Lecturer in Pastoral Care and Counselling. She has been course leader for the Diploma in Pastoral Counselling since that time. Alongside her training role, she carries a small client load. She is married and has two daughters.

David Lyall was formerly minister of a new housing area parish in Ayrshire, and then a hospital chaplain in Edinburgh. He is now Senior Lecturer in the Department of Christian Ethics and Practical Theology in the University of Edinburgh. For several years he was Secretary of the International Council on Pastoral Care and Counselling, and is a former editor of *Contact: The Interdisciplinary Journal of Pastoral Studies*.

Gordon Lynch is the editor of this book. At the time of writing, he lectures in counselling within the Department of Health and Community Studies at University College Chester. In 1995, he completed a PhD in the field of pastoral counselling at Birmingham University. He has subsequently published a number of journal articles and book chapters in the areas of pastoral counselling, post-modernism and therapy, and counselling research. He is a practising counsellor, and his work is influenced primarily by psychodynamic theories.

Jessica Rose is a counsellor in private practice. At the time of writing she is Lecturer in Pastoral Psychology at Ripon College, Cuddesdon, where women and men train for ordained ministry in the Church of England, and is a member of the training team of the Oxford Christian Institute for Counselling. She is married with one daughter, and is a member of the Orthodox Church.

Alistair Ross is a Baptist minister, and a part-time lecturer in pastoral counselling at St John's College, Nottingham. He is involved in research and is writing a 'psychodynamic theology' at the Queen's

Foundation, Birmingham. This is a subject he began to explore in his book *Evangelicals in Exile: Wrestling with Theology and the Unconscious* (DLT). He is a pastoral counsellor in private practice and is currently working on a book about counselling skills for church and faith community workers. His previous research was on Frank Lake and clinical theology.

ACKNOWLEDGEMENTS

I am grateful to Peter van de Kasteele, Director of the Clinical Theology Association, for giving permission for David Lyall's paper on post-modernism to be reprinted in this volume. This paper was originally delivered as the 1995 Frank Lake Memorial Lecture, and is still in print as one of the Clinical Theology Association's Lingdale Papers. Further information on this can be obtained from the Clinical Theology Association, St Mary's House, Church Westcote, Oxford, OX7 6SF.

INTRODUCTION

Gordon Lynch

Clinical Counselling in Pastoral Settings is part of a new series of books published by Routledge which seeks to explore the practice of counselling in various contexts. Other titles in the series consider the significance of settings, such as primary care, and higher and further education, for the work of the counsellor. A fundamental assumption within this series is that the nature and process of therapeutic work is inextricably bound up with the context in which the counsellor is working. Thus, rather than seeing counselling practice simply as the application of generalised therapeutic theories, this series takes the view that effective counsellors shape their practice in response to the particular context of their work. The skilled counsellor should therefore be able to make use of those aspects of their context which promote therapeutic change and growth, as well as being aware of aspects of their context that are harmful to their clients' psychological well-being.

This series has been prepared with practitioners very much in mind. Each book seeks to explore relevant issues for those working, or thinking of working, in various counselling settings. It is intended not only that readers should gain theoretical insights into the influence of particular contexts on counselling work, but that the books in the series should also explore specific examples of counselling practice in these contexts. Whilst some individual chapters inevitably lend themselves to more theoretical discussions, authors in the series have generally tried to weave case examples into their chapters to make the practical relevance of their material clear.

In certain respects, however, *Clinical Counselling in Pastoral Settings* is an unusual book within this series. The term 'pastoral settings' covers a much wider range of specific counselling contexts than any of the other titles. Pastoral counsellors work in settings as diverse as local parishes or congregations, independent pastoral counselling agencies, private practice, or educational, medical, industrial or prison chaplaincies. Clearly,

1

each of these specific contexts presents its own distinctive qualities and challenges. Rather than focusing in detail on each of these specific contexts, as Editor I decided to invite a range of chapters on issues that would be of more general concern to pastoral counsellors. The content of these is summarised below.

The definition of pastoral counselling that I have brought to this book is that it is counselling practice which is explicitly shaped by a particular religious tradition or which is explicitly associated with a particular religious institution or organisation. Whilst many of the writers in this book acknowledge or assume this definition, it is important to recognise that even this broad definition can be contested. In the concluding chapter, John Foskett makes a cogent case for seeing pastoral counselling more as a kind of attitude within human relationships than a formalised type of therapeutic work associated with religious groups or traditions.

Whilst my definition of pastoral counselling is inclusive of different types of religious tradition and organisation, the authors in this book are generally informed by the Christian tradition. To explore pastoral counselling only in Christian contexts has certain advantages for this book in that it gives it a consistent focus that it might otherwise have lacked. Pastoral counsellors whose work is shaped by other faith traditions may feel that some of the content of this book is less relevant to them as a consequence of this, however. My hope is that the discussions within this book of issues such as pastoral counselling and prayer, the appropriate boundaries of pastoral counselling, and transference and countertransference in pastoral counselling will be of direct relevance not only to Christian pastoral counsellors. Where pastoral counsellors from other faith traditions find that the content of this book is less relevant to their own practice, then my further hope is that this book will serve as an invitation and stimulus for future published work which addresses their experience and concerns more adequately.

The focus of this book on Christian pastoral counselling is timely. Christian pastoral counselling in Britain is at a crucial stage in its development. We are currently witnessing the passing of a generation who had a pioneering role in the development of pastoral counselling in the 1960s and 1970s through organisations such as the Clinical Theology Association, the Association for Pastoral Care and Counselling and the Westminster Pastoral Foundation. The work of the many people who were involved in the creation and development of these organisations has been invaluable, and the wider counselling movement in Britain owes a great (and usually unacknowledged) debt to them. With the passing of this 'first wave', however, the future of Christian pastoral counselling in Britain is unclear.

At present, there are a number of different organisations in which Christian pastoral counsellors are involved. In addition to those already mentioned, the Association for Christian Counsellors and the Acorn Christian Healing Trust also represent significant networks of people involved in pastoral counselling work. Whilst this diversity of organisations allows individual pastoral counsellors to be involved in groups that they find congenial in terms of their theological and therapeutic outlook, there is also a price to be paid here in terms of the fragmentation of the Christian pastoral counselling scene. Unlike counsellors in other contexts, such as educational, medical or work-place settings, there is no single organisation which all Christian pastoral counsellors recognise in Britain as their lead body. The absence of such a national body arguably leads to considerable waste both in terms of ineffective communication among Christian pastoral counsellors and in terms of duplication of effort with, for example, systems of accreditation. More significantly, however, the absence of such a lead body has a detrimental effect upon the ability of Christian pastoral counsellors to have a clear voice in the wider counselling scene and upon the ability of the Christian pastoral counselling movement to maintain any core identity. This lack of voice and lack of a core identity are perhaps the greatest threats to Christian pastoral counsellors being able in the future to deliver a useful service to their clients that is valued both by their peers in the wider counselling profession and by society more generally.

Whether the political issues that give rise to this fragmentation will be addressed is something that lies primarily in the hands of those involved in existing pastoral counselling organisations. Where, I hope, this book will make a contribution is in raising issues that are of concern to all those involved in the practice of Christian pastoral counselling. For if this book succeeds in stimulating a debate about the nature of pastoral counselling in Christian contexts that transcends existing organisational boundaries, then this may eventually be of use in the development of a clearer identity to the wider Christian pastoral counselling movement in Britain.

The issues explored in this book have been chosen in the belief that the practice of pastoral counselling is influenced by the interaction of three different factors. These are the cultural context in which the pastoral counselling takes place, the religious tradition that informs the work of the pastoral counsellor, and contemporary understanding of the therapeutic process and of the appropriate structure of the counselling relationship. Individual chapters within the book seek to explore aspects of each of these three different factors.

The first two chapters explore key issues concerning the cultural context of contemporary pastoral counselling. In the first chapter, David Lyall explores the significance of postmodern culture for Christian pastoral counselling. In this chapter Lyall summarises key aspects of our postmodern culture and argues that this culture is one that encourages the growth of counselling. He goes on to make a case for different religious traditions influencing pastoral counselling practice in distinctive and diverse ways, and gives some outline of how the Christian tradition may inform counselling practice. In chapter 2, Emmanuel Lartey discusses the implications for practising pastoral counselling in a multi-cultural context. Here, Lartey argues for the importance of recognising the cultural emphases that are present in all forms of counselling practice, and contrasts broad assumptions with Western, Asian and African cultures that are relevant to therapeutic work. He then goes on to explore different approaches to pastoral counselling work within a multi-cultural context, and makes a strong case for an inter-cultural approach to pastoral counselling which recognises human commonalities as well as cultural and individual differences.

The next two chapters explore how religious resources may inform the work of the pastoral counsellor. In chapter 3, Alistair Ross discusses how religious tradition can play a constructive role in pastoral counselling work. Focusing on the Jewish and Christian traditions, Ross proposes that counselling relationships conducted in religious contexts are valuable in that they provide a space in which clients can interrogate these traditions in order to find some meaning within their experience. In this counselling context, the answers to these questions emerge through the living medium of the counselling relationship and this process can be understood as a form of divine revelation. It is such answers, or indeed the ability to accept that there are no clear answers, that represent a source of hope and salvation within individuals' lives. In chapter 4, Jessica Rose explores the place of prayer in the work of the pastoral counsellor. Here, Rose considers the constructive role that prayer can play within the therapeutic process, as well as the dilemmas and tensions associated with prayer in a counselling context. The place of prayer in sustaining the work of the pastoral counsellor is also discussed.

The following three chapters in the book explore pastoral counselling work from the perspective of contemporary understandings of the appropriate boundaries of therapeutic work and of the nature of the therapeutic process. In chapter 5, Alan Boyd and I introduce the notion of the 'therapeutic frame' as the system of boundaries that make it possible for the counselling relationship to function as a containing and reflective environment for the counsellor and client. The role of the therapeutic frame is discussed, and it is suggested that an understanding of the frame can help practitioners to distinguish between pastoral counselling and pastoral care relationships. Difficulties associated with establishing an appropriate therapeutic frame when working in pastoral settings are also considered. In chapter 6, I continue this exploration of boundary issues in more detail by focusing on the specific issue of dual relationships in pastoral counselling. In this chapter, I outline both the significant disadvantages of dual relationships for counselling work and the problems with making an outright prohibition of all such dual relationships. I go on to suggest that pastoral practitioners need to develop a reflective approach to the problem of dual relationships which will hopefully enable the best interests of clients to be served. In chapter 7, Barrie Hinksman explores the issue of transference and countertransference in the work of the pastoral counsellor. Having given a theoretical overview of the phenomena of transference and counter-transference, Hinksman goes on to consider some distinctive forms of both positive and negative transference that may emerge when the client works with a counsellor who is explicitly associated with a religious institution or tradition. Implications for pastoral counsellors, both in terms of how they may appropriately work with their clients' transference and in terms of specific forms of countertransference that may arise for them in their work, are also discussed.

The final two chapters address other key issues that pastoral counsellors face in their work. In chapter 8, Ruth Layzell describes how pastoral counsellors may respond therapeutically to those who have experienced abuse in religious settings. In this chapter, Layzell offers a broad definition of abuse and discusses the specific processes and effects associated with abuse in a religious context. She then goes on to offer an overview of how pastoral counsellors may work therapeutically with individuals who have experienced such abuse. Finally, in chapter 9, John Foskett takes a broad overview of the promise and challenges associated with contemporary pastoral counselling. Here, Foskett argues for the importance of an approach to pastoral counselling which is concerned with hearing and keeping in mind the experience of the unheard minority, rather than being concerned with issues of professional consolidation. The path that Foskett advocates is one characterised by openness and uncertainty, in which genuine encounter with others becomes a possibility. This approach demands a willingness to move beyond familiar frameworks and beliefs, but offers the promise of a creative and more authentic existence in which we may understand more fully what it means to be human.

I am very grateful to each of the authors for the work that they have put into these chapters. Within the book as a whole there are certain recurrent themes, and there are also some important tensions between the views of different authors. I believe that such disagreement and debate is invaluable to the ongoing development of the pastoral counselling movement. This collection of chapters is therefore offered in a spirit of encouraging further reflection and discussion among those involved in counselling work in pastoral settings. I think it is important that throughout these chapters there is a recognition of both the value of religious resources in promoting human well-being and of the harm that religious traditions and institutions can cause to people. If this book serves to stimulate pastoral counsellors to draw upon what is healthy about the context in which they work, and to resist what is unhealthy, then it will have served a useful purpose.

1

PASTORAL COUNSELLING IN A POSTMODERN CONTEXT

David Lyall

Introduction

I must begin with a word of explanation – and perhaps of reassurance. I am not a philosopher and so this chapter will not be concerned with philosophical analysis. That lies beyond my competence. But while I am not a philosopher, I live and move and have my being in a world full of them! And as I listen to the conversation of my academic colleagues, I hear them use a certain kind of language, and I am aware that they are describing concepts and realities which attempt to name and identify certain fundamental changes which are taking place in society. I thought therefore, as I began to look for a theme for this chapter, that it might be an idea to identify the nature of this so-called postmodern society about which my colleagues were talking, to try to tease out what (if anything) it meant in practice and to explore the possible implications for pastoral counselling.

Interestingly, when I had identified this theme as one worthy of exploration, two things happened which persuaded me that my thoughts were not totally idiosyncratic. The first was that John Patton, one of America's leading authorities on pastoral counselling, wrote an article for *Pastoral Psychology* entitled 'Pastoral postmodernism' (see Patton 1994). In this paper he argues that the same kind of so-called 'postmodern critique' currently being brought to bear upon literary texts can also be applied to the 'living human documents' of the pastoral encounter. The second was that I received the programme for the 1995 conference of a group of German pastoral organisations, the theme being 'Pastoral Care and Counselling in Postmodern Time'. It seems, therefore, that both in the United States and in Germany people are beginning to explore the implications of postmodernism for pastoral care and so it is not inappropriate that I should use this chapter to make a contribution to the debate in Britain. I offer this chapter, then, not as a philosophical expert but as a practitioner and a teacher of pastoral care exploring a new set of ideas – and in that spirit I invite you to join me in this journey. But first of all, to define terms.

What is meant by 'postmodern'?

The trouble with a word such as 'postmodern' is that many people use it as though they know what they are talking about, but when you begin to look for a precise definition you find that common understandings are hard to come by. Indeed, for some the term is already passé. In his monograph entitled *Postmodernity* Barry Smart (1993) writes:

> Postmodernity. What is it? What was it? When was it? Were you there? Amused? Bemused? Convinced? Disdainful? Enchanted? Irritated or just plain indifferent? For some, the grazers and zappers of the analytical domain, it is already a question of what postmodernity *was*. References to post-post-modernity suggest that it is a time which is already past. . . . More interesting in my view are the contributions which con-sider postmodernity to be a matter of current concern, an idea that may have a bearing on our understanding and experience of present conditions; postmodernity as a contemporary social, cultural and political condition. Postmodernity as a form of life, a form of reflection upon and a response to the accumulating signs of the limits and limitations of modernity.
>
> (1993: 12)

It is in that last phrase, 'a response to the accumulating signs of the limits and limitations of modernity', that we catch a glimpse of what this debate is all about. The basic thesis is that we are now experiencing a major shift in our understanding of how things are. Until recently we have understood ourselves as living in 'modern times'. These modern times have, in fact, been with us for a long time. They have their roots in the rationality of post-Newtonian science and in the ideas of the Enlightenment of the seventeenth and eighteenth centuries. The key ideas of modernism, ideas which have shaped our thinking until comparatively recently, have been a belief in science, reason, rationality, education and the inevitability of progress And all this accompanied by the marginalisation and the privatisation of religious faith.

8

The postmodern thesis is that all this is changing, that we are now moving into an era in which the certainties of Newtonian science and Cartesian philosophy no longer hold fast. If, however, the world-view which flows from the Enlightenment is breaking down, how then may we characterise the present situation, this 'postmodern condition', this cultural milieu in which we seek to exercise our various ministries of pastoral care and counselling? It has to be recognised that the answer to that question is complex and often full of self-contradiction. But it has also to be recognised that that is precisely the point! There are now no commonly held understandings of how things are. This is certainly true of the contemporary religious scene, which constitutes at least part of the context of pastoral care and counselling.

The French philosopher Jean-François Lyotard (1984), in his book *The Postmodern Condition*, argues that there is no longer any 'grand story' which can claim universal assent. Neither religion nor politics can provide any universal theory, any overarching belief system, to which the majority of people can give their allegiance. The extent to which this is true is debatable. Certainly, institutional religion, as far as the mainline churches are concerned, appears to be in decline. Yet there are contrary indications as well. Fundamentalism in religion, and not only in Christianity, is on the march. And who would have thought that in the last decade of the scientific century that there would have been a burgeoning interest in spirituality? In methods ranging from New Age to Ignatian, people are searching for personal meaning. There is a free market in religion, and in this 'pick and mix' culture, people are putting together their own packages, finding a religious or spiritual stance which makes sense from perspectives shaped by the stories of their own lives. In the absence of 'grand stories', only the local, personal stories make sense.

In *Cosmopolis: The Hidden Agenda of Modernity*, Stephen Toulmin (1990) identifies four characteristics of so-called 'modernism' which in turn have been reversed by the advent of postmodernism. A central part of my argument is that if Toulmin is right, then his thesis has important implications for pastoral care and counselling. His argument is that in the seventeenth century four movements took place which until very recently have dominated intellectual discourse.

First, there was a movement **from the Oral to the Written**. Rhetoric was out; logic was in. In premodern times (and by that I mean pre-seventeenth century), rhetoric, the skill of debate, of argumentation, was highly valued. But in the modern age, rhetoric fell into disrepute (note how we use the phrase 'mere rhetoric'). What was wanted was not argumentation but proof. And with the emphasis upon logical proof

9

rather than convincing argument, there was an inevitable shift from the spoken word to the written word.

Second, there was a movement **from the Particular to the Universal**. Prior to the seventeenth century, debate in the fields of ethics and law centred on the study of cases. The Jesuits were famed for their casuistry, their analysis of specific 'cases of conscience'. With modernity came the search for a more universal, abstract ethical theory divorced from the 'messiness' of particular situations. It was assumed that what was good and just could be stated in terms of what was timeless and universal. General principles were in, particular cases were out.

Third, there was a movement **from the Local to the General**. Prior to the Age of Modernity, humanists found their sources for reflection in ethnography, history and geography, the raw data of which was to be acquired through the study of what was happening in specific local situations. General theories of human behaviour were built up inductively from a study of specific human action. Modern philosophy, beginning with Descartes, reversed this trend. While he saw the curiosity of historians and ethnographers as a pardonable human trait, he taught that philosophical understanding never comes from accumulating experience of particular individuals and specific cases, Philosophy was concerned with abstract principles which would provide a unifying framework explaining the diversity of particular local situations.

Fourth, there was a movement **from the Timely to the Timeless**. In premodern times, in medicine and in law there was a consideration as to whether an action was timely. Was that the right thing to do *at that time*? It was recognised that a decision might be right at a given time in a given situation but that the same action might be totally inappropriate some time later. With the advent of modern philosophy all that changed and the aim was to bring to light the permanent structures underlying all the changing phenomena of the world.

Thus, the advent of modernism, that philosophical understanding of the world which reigned supreme for three hundred years from the seventeenth century until comparatively recently, brought with it an understanding of the world which exalted the written, the universal, the general and the timeless at the expense of the oral, the particular, the local and the timely. That is the first part of Toulmin's argument. The second part, and it is this which I believe is of significance for contemporary pastoral counselling, is that with the advent of postmodernity, these four movements of modernity have been put into reverse or at least broadened to include the oral, the particular, the local and the timely.

First, **the Return to the Oral**. Toulmin argues that over the past twenty years or so, there has been a concern among language scholars with forms of communication other than the written word, There is a new or renewed interest in oral communication. An emphasis upon 'the text' is giving way to an awareness of the context of communication. Recent years have seen a growing awareness of narrative, of story, and as often as not, this is communicated through the spoken word as much as the written word.

Second, **the Return to the Particular**. Toulmin argues that with casuistry having been thrown out about three hundred years ago, that movement has now been reversed, with a fresh emphasis upon considering general ethical principles in the light of specific cases. If we look at recent ethical discussions in the public domain we see the truth of this statement, particularly in the area of medical ethics. The case of Tony Bland raised the broader issue of the appropriate treatment of patients in a persistent vegetative state; the case of the ten-year-old girl dying of cancer with a very slight chance of benefiting from treatment costing £75,000 raised the more general issue of resource allocation. So too, in the political domain, largely because of media interest, general discussion relating to the private morality of public figures is generated through the publicity given to specific cases.

Third, **the Return to the Local**. Whereas modernism discounted the importance of the local context as a contribution to general understanding, in recent research across a whole range of intellectual endeavours, ethnographic and historical studies have become important. There is a new awareness of the significance of context. The ways in which ethical issues are perceived in Protestant Northern Europe is sometimes different from those in the Catholic heartland of the Mediterranean. Anthropology and history and geography have to be taken seriously.

Finally, **the Return to the Timely**. Toulmin argues that there is now an awareness that it is more important that actions should be right in the *here and now* rather than be eternally valid. He illustrates this by reference to clinical medicine, which must go beyond the rules of 'natural science' to the kind of practice where physicians bring their carefully digested experience to decide what is best for *this* patient at *this particular time*.

What has all this to do with pastoral care and counselling? If Toulmin's analysis is right and contemporary culture, which has been described as 'postmodern', does now value the oral, the particular, the local and the timely, then I believe that this does have profound implications for our understanding of pastoral counselling. In the remainder of this chapter I wish to argue three points, all of which I think follow from the above, brief analysis of the postmodern context. My three theses are as follows:

1 The growth of the counselling movement itself is understandable in the context of postmodern society.
2 In the context of the postmodern world of competing narratives, the Christian narrative has its own integrity and value in relation to pastoral counselling.
3 In the context of the counselling relationship, the Christian narrative may be expressed in ways that stir the imagination (i.e. parabolically and poetically).

1 Counselling in the postmodern context

It may be no more than coincidence that the phenomenal growth in the counselling movement has taken place in the past thirty years, during the period of time that has been labelled as 'postmodern'. Yet if we accept Toulmin's analysis of contemporary culture with his emphasis upon the oral, the particular, the local and the timely, we cannot fail to see that these emphases are ones which create in our society a climate favourable to the growth of counselling in all its forms.

If it is nothing else, counselling is a form of oral communication. It is a helping relationship that depends upon people talking to one another. The event is structured in such a way as to allow talking to take place in an unimpeded way. The talking is prized, guarded and fenced around, with maximum oral communication taking place within the counselling relationship, nothing of that communication being spread abroad beyond itself, save for the purposes of supervision, another oral event designed specifically to enhance understanding of the first. Even when the event is written about, in a process report or a 'verbatim', the aim is to capture as fully as possible what was said. I think we can take it that counselling is part of an oral culture.

There is also in counselling an emphasis upon the particular. It does not work unless counsellees are prepared to be specific about the details of their own stories. The success of counselling depends upon helping people to say, 'This is me,' and they must be specific primarily about themselves rather than their problems. As John Patton (1990: 894) has written, pastoral counselling 'involves assisting persons to move from talking generally about themselves and specifically about their problems to talking specifically about themselves and generally about their problems'. Counselling depends upon helping people understand and accept the uniqueness of their own lives and to catch a vision of their own potential for transformation and growth. For the counsellor the process involves hearing the meanings which are unique to the client in the midst of many similar stories, avoiding the temptation to label people as examples of more general problems.

When we come to Toulmin's emphasis upon 'the local', I believe we find this reflected in the current interest in the context of counselling. Indeed, the very series of which this book is a part indicates the growing awareness of the influence of context upon counselling theory and practice. There is also an awareness of the significance of context in the rapidly developing international pastoral care and counselling movement. Alongside the commonality of interest, the dependence upon the same literature, the flirtation with the same secular therapies, there are also features of pastoral care unique to individual cultures and countries. Padmasani Gallup (1992), an Indian woman highly trained in the skills of the North American pastoral counselling movement, presented a case at a recent international congress which illustrated this point well. She spoke of a case of a Hindu woman, married with two children, who was abused both emotionally and physically by her husband. Many of us might take the view that a possible aim of counselling might be to explore with the woman whether or not she wanted to stay in that intolerable situation. For Padmasani Gallup that choice did not exist. Since it is the status of the Hindu woman who is divorced or separated which is intolerable, for her the counselling task must be to enable the woman to stay in the marriage and try to change the dynamics of that relationship. Her point is that the context, the local situation, must have an impact upon the counselling relationship.

Nor need I dwell unduly upon the importance of the timely in the counselling relationship. In evaluating counsellor responses to what the client said, we do not ask whether the response contains eternal, timeless truth (even if it is expressed in the words of Holy Scripture) but whether it is the right thing to say to that client *at this moment*. The emphasis is upon being present to the other, upon immediacy and empathy and congruence (and I speak of these qualities assuming that they are deemed to be important irrespective of the model of counselling or pastoral care involved).

So, then, if Toulmin's analysis is right, and postmodern society is characterised by an emphasis upon the oral, the particular, the local and the timely, then it should not surprise us that this has been a rich cultural soil in which counselling could take root and flourish. Indeed, it would have been surprising if it had not done so. I am arguing, in the first place, therefore that there is a kind of 'fit' between postmodern society and the self-understanding of the counselling movement.

What are the implications of postmodernism for the distinctively pastoral ministries of the Christian church? I earlier referred to the work of Jean-François Lyotard, who, in *The Postmodern Condition*, has argued that there is no longer any 'grand story' which can claim universal assent. What then is the place of the Christian story in relation to the contemporary counselling movement? To return to an old question but in a different context – is there such a thing as *pastoral* counselling and what is it in a postmodern context?

2 Christian narrative and pastoral counselling

While many philosophers would regard Lyotard's position as extreme, there is no doubt that the Christian story does not command universal assent. And even among those counsellors who at a personal level would wish to identify themselves as belonging within the Christian tradition, there are very different views regarding how their own faith relates to the practice of counselling. On the one hand, there are many counsellors, especially those working in secular organisations, whose lives are enriched by their own religious experience but who would find it totally inappropriate that this should find any explicit expression in their counselling. On the other hand, there are the rapidly increasing numbers of counsellors who are much more explicit in their use of Christian words and meanings in their counselling. It seems to me that a central question in pastoral counselling remains the relationship of the Christian story to the practice of counselling. This is important, internally, as part of the dialogue within the Christian community because of the great diversity of views held. And it is important externally as we seek to exercise a ministry of pastoral counselling in an increasingly pluralistic culture where the competing narratives of other religious traditions are vying for attention.

The sub-plot here of course is the discussion about the relationship between the different religious traditions and the nature of religious truth, far bigger issues than can be dealt within the confines of this chapter. In a paper, 'Theology and the faiths', John McIntyre (1988), formerly Professor of Divinity at Edinburgh University, explores the different ways in which Christianity has tried to relate to the other great world religions. He sets out in some detail the traditional arguments which have governed the relationship between Christianity and other faiths within the three broad categories of *exclusivism*, *inclusivism* and *pluralism*. Ultimately, McIntyre takes his stand on what is essentially an exclusivist position. He quotes his own immediate predecessor, the late Professor John Baillie (1929: 123), who wrote that 'religious judgements, being what they are and making claim to objective truth as they undoubtedly do, it is psychologically an impossible feat, as well as logically a self-contradictory desire, *not* to make one's own fundamental religious convictions the criterion of religious truth'.

This is not, however, the old-fashioned exclusivism which led to inter-faith anathematisation. On the contrary, because disagreements have been made explicit, the tolerance that must be expressed in the midst of the disagreement becomes all the more important. What is required is discursive dialogue where the attempt to understand the beliefs of others is balanced by genuine confrontation and a desire to persuade the other as in other arenas of human discourse such as politics and philosophy.

What has all this to do with pastoral care and counselling? I wish to argue that in a pluralistic, postmodern context pastoral care and counselling find their true identity and integrity in relation to the Christian narrative. In the development of pastoral counselling in the twentieth century, we see a reflection of concurrent theological development. From its early dependence upon Rogerian and other secular therapists to the recent rapid expansion of Christian counselling we see reflected the influences of mid-century liberalism and late-century conservative evangelicalism. It was perhaps inevitable that in the early need to achieve professional credibility, the secular therapies were the controlling influence upon the development of pastoral counselling, with the result of this being a consequent detachment from its roots within Christian ministry. The result of this has been twofold. On the one hand, there has been the emergence of a *pastoral* counselling movement very much at home in a pluralistic context. On the other hand, there has been the development of a *Christian* counselling movement which fits very comfortably with the older exclusive model of relating to persons of a different faith or belief system. This in turn has led to a pastoral counselling movement, theologically impoverished, which is cut off from its roots within the ministry of the people of God, and has no clear identity in dialogue with other therapies. And in the absence of a pastoral counselling movement with clear Christian identity we have seen the development of a Christian counselling movement which can sometimes seem to be *over*-identified with one interpretation of the Gospel.

I wish to argue that, amidst the competing therapies of postmodern pluralism, pastoral counselling will make its distinctive contribution to the care and growth of people when it finds its identity in the narratives of the Judaeo-Christian tradition. When pastoral counselling seeks to explain itself – to itself and to the wider psychotherapeutic community

– it must engage in the discursive dialogue of John McIntyre's modified exclusivism, where an honest attempt to understand the perspective of others is balanced by an equally honest attempt to explain itself in terms of its own story. In the 'free market' of a plural society, pastoral counselling based upon the Christian narrative has its own integrity and, I believe, can make a valuable contribution to wider society.

Let me make clear what I am **not** saying at present. I am not at present saying anything about the **content** of the pastoral conversation, or about **how** this Christian identity manifests itself in the counselling relationship. I will address this matter in the third section of this chapter. For the time being I am focusing only upon the roots, the identity, the self-understanding of those who claim to be pastoral counsellors.

Christian identity is formed by biblical narrative. It is the stories of the Old and New Testaments which shape our understanding as Christians, as people engaged in ministry, and as pastoral counsellors. In the story of Creation, we have an affirmation of women and men created in the image of God; in the story of their creation as male and female and in the blessing of that creation, we have an affirmation not only of their humanity but of their sexuality. In the story of the Fall and of the sub-sequent, pursuing love of God in the Old Testament we are confronted with a God with a boundless love for his creation. For the pastoral counsellor, acceptance is no mere counselling technique which has been discovered empirically to facilitate growth. Rather, it is an expression of the acceptance that is integral to the nature and love of God.

Central to the Christian narrative is the biblical account of the Incarnation, the story of the Word becoming flesh and dwelling among us full of grace and truth. The Christian God is one who identifies with and enters into the suffering of humankind. For the counsellor whose identity is shaped by the Christian narrative this has several implications. Again, we must affirm that empathy, like acceptance, is no mere psychological technique. Empathy, the attempt to enter into the mindset of those we seek to help, and the communication of that empathy, point to – and indeed are expressions of – the God who has accommodated himself to us in the frailness of our humanity and who in the midst of that frailty has revealed his glory. A second implication of the Incarnation is that the communication of Christian truth is relational and not propositional. The Word became flesh and dwelt among us . . . full of grace and truth. What is not true for the pastoral counsellor, what cannot, must not, be true are the words of the Scottish poet Edwin Muir (1956) as he meditated upon the worst features of Calvinisn: 'The Word made flesh is here made word again.' For counsellors whose identity is shaped by the Christian narrative, what we *are* in our pastoral relationships with people will take precedence over what we *say*. The content of the pastoral conversation will always have its own importance but only in the context of a pastoral relationship which is itself an embodiment of the Gospel.

The story of the Cross and Resurrection is also central to the formation of Christian identity and must, I maintain, shape the self-understanding of the pastoral counsellor. Whatever view we hold of the human condition, to counsel with our identity shaped by these narratives means at least two things. On the one hand, it is to see ourselves and others as responsible before God; it is to understand alienation – our own and those for whom we care – as having a dimension which transcends the human. But it is also, on the other hand, to counsel in the belief that, whatever else Resurrection means, there is the possibility of fresh beginnings, of hope arising from the ashes of despair; it is to counsel in the belief that there is no human folly which cannot be forgiven, no human grief which cannot in some measure be consoled, no human darkness into which a glimmer of light cannot break through.

Again, let me make it quite clear what I am not doing at present. I am not saying anything about the content of the pastoral conversation; I am not making a plea that the language of counselling should be dressed up in what Seward Hiltner once called 'the common currencies of the faith'. I am not arguing that in the pastoral context there are magical solutions which short-circuit the painful growth which is often integral to the counselling process. What I am arguing is that amidst the psychotherapeutic pluralism of our postmodern culture, a culture of competing ideologies, we need to affirm the identity of the counselling which is offered in the pastoral context, an identity which, I have argued, is shaped uniquely by the Christian narrative.

Much confusion about the nature of pastoral counselling has been caused, I believe, by a failure to separate an understanding of the theology of pastoral counselling from views regarding the content of the pastoral conversation. I have so far attempted to outline the basis for the former with an identity rooted in the Christian narrative. My task now is to explore how this identity may impinge upon the counselling process in a manner that respects both the integrity of the pastoral counsellor and the autonomy of the client.

3 Pastoral communication as poetic and parabolic

I wish to argue that in pastoral counselling there are modes of communication which, while inevitably involving the use of words, transcend the meaning of the words themselves. In this sense pastoral communication has a parabolic nature. There are significant parallels between ways of interpreting the parables and our understanding of pastoral care. There was a time when the parables were seen as moral tales, as stories with a message which was self-evident; and this was paralleled by an understanding of pastoral care as the giving of good advice, of a pastor of wisdom and experience guiding 'his' flock. More recent ways of interpreting the parables see them as stories of ordinary things with the power to disclose the nature of reality. Paul Ricoeur writes:

> The first thing which may strike us is that the parables are radically profane stories – there are no gods, no demons, no angels, no miracles, no time before time, as in the creation stories, not even founding events as in the Creation account. . . . Instead they tell about ordinary people doing ordinary things; selling and buying, letting down a net into the sea, and so on. Here resides the initial paradox; on the one hand these stories are . . . narratives of normalcy – but on the other hand it is the Kingdom of God which is said to be like this. The Paradox is that *the extraordinary is like the ordinary*.
>
> (Capps 1981: 157)

It was Donald Capps (1981) in his *Biblical Approaches to Pastoral Counseling* who first wrote of the use of parables in the context of marriage counselling. His thesis was that the counsellee's narrative had a metaphorical level and that in pastoral conversation this metaphorical level is understood as the activity of God. He argues that:

> the ultimate focus of this counseling, the activity of God, is filtered through stories of ordinary, mundane, 'secular' experience. In the parables, there are no direct references to God, and there is no basis for identifying God with any of the protagonists in the stories, including the father in the parable of the Prodigal Son. . . . Whether God is actually referred to in the conversation depends upon the circumstances, not on the supposition that conversation without God is somehow less than pastoral. But it is essential that the conversation be sensitive to how God is acting in the counselee's situation.
>
> (1981: 202)

I wish to argue that it is not simply that the pastoral *conversation* which must be interpreted metaphorically and parabolically but that it is the pastoral *relationship* itself which has a parabolic character. It is the pastoral relationship which is a sign of the kingdom, a metaphor of grace. I have argued above that pastoral counselling finds its unique identity in the biblical narrative; it is this that sets the context for pastoral counselling. Counselling rooted in this narrative will itself point beyond itself to the God who is true to Himself in creation and redemption, who identifies with us in our weakness and comes to us in the depths of our despair embodying hope and new life. Context is important; context is constituted by narrative, and the narrative identity of the community of faith will find expression implicitly as well as explicitly in the pastoral care which is offered within that community.

Another way of stating this may be to claim that, at its best, pastoral counselling possesses something even more potent than the disclosive power of the parabolic. It also has the power to evoke within the imagination new possibilities for the future. In this sense good pastoral counselling has to it a poetic quality. In a chapter entitled 'Beyond the core conditions', Brian Thorne (1991), a British person-centred counsellor, writes of the need to be 'sensitive to the moments in therapy when prose gives way to poetry' and goes on to write of counselling situations where 'empathy and its expression often leads into a world where language becomes even more richly expressive and where the practice of therapy assumes the characteristic of an art form' (1991: 83).

Poetry is an art form that stirs the imagination and enables us to think in new ways. Poetry uses words but not with the same logic as prose; indeed, it is sometimes in the illogical juxtaposition of conflicting ideas that fresh insights are engendered. In their *Mutative Metaphors in Psychotherapy*, Murray Cox and Alice Theilgaard (1987) write:

> Plato's Symposium provides us with the primary source for the term *poiesis*. It is the process of 'calling into existence something which was not there before'. Heidegger refers to it as a 'bringing forth', using the term in its widest sense. He thought of 'poetry' which required the poet but ... he also thought of a poetry without the poets – the blooming of a blossom, the coming-out of a butterfly from a cocoon, the plummeting of a waterfall when the snow begins to melt. The last two analogies underline the fact that Heidegger's example is a threshold occasion, a moment of ectasis when something moves away from its standing as one thing to become another.
>
> (1987: 23)

In *Absolute Truths*, the last of her six novels about the Church of England, Susan Howatch (1995) chronicles the transformation which takes place in the life of Charles Ashworth, Bishop of Starbridge. Ashworth understands his vocation as a theologian and a bishop as a calling to counteract with the 'absolute truth' of the Gospel what he perceives to be the theological heresies and relativistic moralities of the 1960s. He is portayed as being less than sensitive to his nearest and dearest. A turning point in the story comes immediately after his wife's sudden death when he finds and begins to read his wife's spiritual diary, a document that he did not know existed. As he reads, he begins to realise that he never fully knew his wife, never listened to her struggles, never understood what was going on as this odd, not very religious woman took the risk of forming a prayer group for women. But as he read, he became aware, as he had not been aware before, of his wife's experience, of the butterfly coming out from the cocoon, of the plummeting waterfall as the snow melted. And this became for him a threshold occasion, an ecstatic moment as he began this own long journey of personal transformation.

Pastoral care, at its best, has this poetic dimension. Steeped in biblical narrative, its central themes are those of death and life, of despair and hope, of suffering and resurrection, and the transformative power of the Gospel. In their freedom to draw upon the resources of the Gospel and in their equal freedom to remain silent; in their freedom to conform to the rules of good secular therapy and in their freedom (poetically as it were) to allow the transformative power of the pastoral relationship itself to stir the imagination, pastoral counsellors can enable their care of people to become moments of ecstasis, parables of grace, when those whom they counsel find a new perspective and move on to the truth both about themselves and of the love of God.

REFERENCES

Baillie, J. (1929) *The Interpretation of Religion*, Edinburgh: T&T Clark.
Capps, D. (1981) *Biblical Approaches to Pastoral Counseling*, Philadelphia: Westminster.
Cox, M. and Theilgaard, A. (1987) *Mutative Metaphors in Psychotherapy*, London: Tavistock.
Gallup, P. (1992) ' "Subham": the concept of wholeness in pastoral counseling in the Hindu cultural context', in O. Strange (ed.), *Pastoral Care and Context*, Amsterdam: VU University Press, 65–79.
Howatch, S. (1995) *Absolute Truths*, London: HarperCollins.

Lyotard, J.-F. (1984) *The Postmodern Condition*, Manchester: Manchester University Press.

McIntyre, J. (1988) 'Theology and the faiths', unpublished paper given at St Andrew's University Theological Society.

Muir, E. (1956) *One Foot in Eden*, London: Faber.

Patton, J. (1990) 'Personal story, symbol and myth in pastoral care', in R. Hunter (ed.) *Dictionary of Pastoral Care and Counseling*, Nashville: Abingdon, 893–4.

—— (1994) 'Pastoral postmodernism: a challenge to reclaiming our texts', *Pastoral Psychology*, 43(1): 29–41.

Smart, B. (1993) *Postmodernity*, London: Routledge.

Thorne, B. (1991) *Person-centred Counselling: Therapeutic and Spiritual Dimensions*, London: Whurr.

Toulmin, S. (1990) *Cosmopolis: The Hidden Agenda of Modernity*, Chicago: University of Chicago Press.

2

PASTORAL COUNSELLING IN MULTI-CULTURAL CONTEXTS

Emmanuel Lartey

Introduction

In order to undertake an adequate exploration of pastoral counselling in multi-cultural contexts it is necessary, first, to seek some understanding of the nature and meaning of pastoral counselling in different cultural contexts. It is important to realise that the roots of pastoral counselling in many cultural contexts lie in the healing and restorative rituals and arts practised by priest-healers in antiquity. The traditional healer often combined the roles of priest, therapist and physician. He or she was the one to whom folk went in times of need or difficulty. Their expectation was usually that the priest-healer would offer words and rites grounded in culture, world-view and belief, which would be effective in bringing relief or else offering meaning in the midst of trauma. The traditional healer, as such, had to be knowledgeable concerning a wide range of physical, emotional, social and cultural phenomena. Down through the years these healing arts have, in the West, become separated into specialities which in many cases have proved antagonistic to or else suspicious of each other's abilities.

Modern-day Western pastoral counsellors may appear very different from their historical predecessors. The understanding of what it is they are engaged in may also be radically different. Nevertheless, it is true that the needs, expectations and desires for relief which propel people into counselling relationships today, share several similar features with those in the past. It is also the case that in virtually all areas of the world currently people seek out others they believe to have some knowledge, expertise or power which they understand might help them in their quest for relief, well-being or meaning in life.

In this chapter we first examine some understandings and meanings of pastoral counselling in different cultural settings. Following this we discuss different forms of pastoral counselling arising out of varied models of multi-cultural societies. The chapter ends with a proposal of an inter-cultural approach which it is believed might offer helpful insights for pastoral counsellors wherever they might be at work.

Pastoral counselling in global perspective

Pastoral counselling can be and has been understood in a variety of ways. I have elsewhere presented five distinct understandings which appear in Western contexts (Lartey 1997: 73–8). (1) There is a secular usage in educational settings in Britain in which 'pastoral' counselling focuses on the welfare or well-being of students and the personal, social, moral and/or developmental issues faced by pupils in school. Pastoral tutors in schools seek, through counselling and other means of communication, to facilitate the personal growth and welfare of their students. (2) There is, at the opposite extreme, the exclusive focus of the term upon the counselling work of ordained clergy. Here, pastoral counselling refers to what the clergy do when they offer guidance or counsel to parishioners or others who seek their help. (3) Pastoral counselling may also refer to counselling with a broadly religious frame of reference. This form of counselling, unlike some other forms, does not equate religious belief or expression with pathology but rather seeks to take into account clients' and counsellors' religious sentiments. (4) Pastoral counselling is also seen as counselling offered within or by a community of faith. In this view, groups or individuals within or else representing a particular faith community work with individuals or groups in accordance with the beliefs of their community's faith. An example of this would be Christian counselling or counselling which seeks to base its theory and practice exclusively on the Bible and the tenets of evangelical Christianity. (5) When counselling focuses on the whole rather than specific aspects of a person's experience (e.g. emotions or cognitive functioning alone), then the qualifier 'pastoral' in pastoral counselling refers to the whole person. Here the pastoral counsellor is concerned for the total well-being of a person mentally, physically, emotionally, spiritually and socially. Such a counsellor may not solely offer everything. They would often work alongside others and have recourse to referral as a means of enabling attention to specific needs. However, their overall aim and hope is for holistic health which ignores or minimises no aspect of this.

23

Wicks and Estadt (1993) edited a book entitled *Pastoral Counseling in a Global Church: Voices from the Field* in which the work of pastoral counsellors from ten different countries, namely Venezuela, Panama, Kenya, Malawi, Zambia, Ghana, Thailand, Korea, Australia and the Netherlands, is presented. What is clear in this text is that all the writers have found it necessary to modify the Western-based training they have received with its assumptions and presuppositions in order to relate in culturally different contexts. The Ghanaian pastoral theologian Ghunney, for example, declares:

> After completing the Masters Program in Pastoral Counseling at Loyola College in Maryland, where I learned many theories in counselling, I returned home to Ghana in West Africa with the hope of practising the theories I had learned in the West. I realised, however, that though the theories I learned were good ones, most of them were not practicable in Ghana. The only way I could succeed in the counselling situations there was to contextualize and graft what I had learned with the Ghanaian culture.
>
> (Ghunney 1993: 82)

Clearly, in different geographical areas and contexts what is needed is the freedom to recognise what is of value in their historic traditions, to reject what after careful contextual and contemporary examination proves ineffective, and to initiate new syntheses out of the blending and clashing of the different cultures which make up most of contemporary societies.

Counselling which has developed in the West, by and large, is individualistic, rationalistic and promotes the self (ego) above all else (Halmos 1965; Lambourne 1974; Wilson 1988). This is in line with a system of thought that is essentially materialistic and which, as such, places the highest value on the acquisition of measurable objects. Colin Lago and Joyce Thompson (1996), in a useful book entitled *Race, Culture and Counselling*, attempt to assist counsellors understand the different underlying philosophies which inform non-Western approaches to helping and counselling. They argue that Western forms of knowledge have tended to be external, the result of counting and measuring with the knowers distancing themselves from the object to be known. On the other hand, Asian conceptual systems tend to emphasise cosmic unity and place much value on the cohesiveness of the group. Both inner and external ways of knowing are important, and the aim is the integration of body, mind and spirit, which are considered to be different aspects of the same oneness (1996: 86).

African systems are often based on a spiritual (or supernatural) and pragmatic ontology which places value on relationality. Knowledge is acquired through intuition and revelation which comes through ritual, symbol and rhythm. The focus of healing and counselling then is the relationship between and among persons whose intrinsic worth is to be found through the network of spiritual and familial relationships within which they are embedded. With regard particularly to African and Caribbean contexts reference has been made, within the context of pastoral counselling, to the fact that religion and views of transcendence are pervasive in all of life. There is little or no separation between a 'sacred' or a 'secular' realm. All life is both sacred and secular. These beliefs are expressed most clearly in rituals which are meant to foster and enhance harmonious relations between humans and the unseen world of ancestors, gods and spirits. Rites and rituals emphasise the importance of symbolic representation and celebration. For most traditional African and Caribbean peoples, dreams have great significance because they may be avenues through which the really important issues of life may be communicated to persons. Attention within this context is paid to a plurality of practitioners of healing arts which include traditional priest-healers, herbalists, ritualists as well as diviners, dancers and creative artists. All creative performers are seen as having a part to play in the processes of healing. The pastoral counsellor is seen as being a part of a community of healers. Life, as such, is experienced and conceptualised in holistic or synthetic ways (Lartey 1993; Mulrain 1995).

Masamba ma Mpolo (Masamba and Nwachuku 1991) argues that illness in Africa is often thought of as having spiritual or else relational causes. This is in line with cosmologies that emphasise the inter-relationships between the seen and the unseen world. As such, illness may be ascribed either to bewitchment, the anger of mistreated and offended spiritual forces, possession by an alien spirit or to broken human relations. Masamba therefore suggests that spiritual means 'even through ecstasy, rituals and symbolic representations' (*ibid.* 28) need to be adopted in helping people deal with their emotional and psychological needs.

Berinyuu (1989) attempts to be deeply rooted in the therapeutic practices and interpretations of the peoples of Africa while dialoguing critically with and attempting to integrate Western forms of healing. He defines a pastoral counsellor in Africa as a 'shepherding divine who carefully guides a sheep through a soft muddy spot' (1989: 12). After an examination of the processes and practices of divination in Africa, Berinyuu proposes that divination as both an 'inspired' and a 'deductive' art could be considered an African form of therapy. His model of the pastoral counsellor is essentially that of one who is adept at harnessing the African 'spirit-filled' universe as well as culturally recognisable symbolic forms of interaction such as storytelling, myths and proverbs, dance, drama and music, in the quest for appropriate responses to the exigencies of life. This view could be said to be representative of or at least to approximate to, in broad terms, an essentially African picture of a pastoral counsellor.

The inclusion of spiritual and cultural resources as pivotal to the work of the counsellor is a distinguishing feature of pastoral counselling. On this reckoning pastoral counsellors may originate from or utilise the resources of any religious or spiritual tradition. We can therefore have Christian pastoral counsellors, Islamic pastoral counsellors, Jewish pastoral counsellors and so on. With this in mind, the work of Abdullah Maynard, who teaches an Islamic counselling course in London, is instructive. In an article in which he introduces Islamic counselling, Maynard writes that it is

> based on the study or science of the self (the nafs – self; nafsiyat – science of the self: *arabic*). But it also goes *beyond* the study of the self to worship; the context of meaning in its absolute form being not limited to the actions of an individual but existing in the relationships between the person, their world and the reason for existence itself.
>
> (Maynard 1998: 22)

Islamic counselling, then, as per Maynard, is about seeing a person in their God-given potential, uplifting or inspiring them through assisting them to see this for themselves and working with them to see the meaning of any situation that they are in and their actions within it. The value of a counsellor is not so much in the fact that they share similar experiences with their clients but rather that they have gained a greater understanding of the self. The main attention in this approach is paid to the self, God and correctly focused action. On the self various faculties are identifiable, including *Al hiss mushtarak* – the faculty of common or unifying sense; *khayal* – the faculty of imagination; *wahm* – the faculty of attributing meaning or value; and *mutafakkira* – the faculty of reflection. Maynard quotes a Sufi teacher, Shaykh Fadhlalla Haeri, appropriately as follows:

> The main purpose of all these inner faculties is to help us relate to our constantly changing world. If our common sense is in a healthy state, our faculty for imagination is reliable, our ability to place values on forms is sound and flexible and our reservoir

of information and memories from the past are constantly updated, we may then reflect in an efficient way. . . . But all of this cannot be confined to an intellectual exercise: it needs to be acted upon for it to be of any use.

(Maynard 1998: 23–4)

From this discussion so far, it is clear that all forms of counselling are inseparable from cultural assumptions and biases, and different cultural systems appropriately find expression in different therapeutic styles and approaches. In view of this, it is reasonable to argue that effective counselling practice involves reflection on the significance of both the counsellor's and the client's cultural world for the therapeutic process. In the next part of this chapter we will critically evaluate different approaches to thinking about counselling and cultural difference that counsellors and other professionals currently adopt.

Models of pastoral counselling in pluralistic places

In this section we will examine four models of working in multi-cultural communities and point out the types of pastoral counselling which flow from such social conceptualisations.

Mono-culturalism

Basic maxim: 'We are all really the same.'
The mono-culturalist basically claims to work in a 'colour-blind, culture-free' way. For such a counsellor little or no attention is paid to differences that arise from cultural or social background. The overriding assumption is that all people in a given situation are basically the same. Most often what such workers accept are the presuppositions of the particular theoretical position which undergirds their approach to counselling. They proceed on the basis of these presuppositions, often with little critique or question. Seldom do they raise the question of cultural 'fit'. As such, they unwittingly insist upon the core values and cultural norms of the particular class or social group represented by the theory they espouse.

Mono-culturalism therefore, despite suggestions to the contrary, is not neutral. Two aspects of this unwitting non-neutrality are apparent. First, it universalises particular sets of norms, values, cultural beliefs and practices. Everyone, regardless of preference or background, is assumed or expected to function in accord with these universals. In this regard the 'white Western' and sub-cultures akin to it are regarded as the norm to which all must conform. In terms of pastoral counselling, the 'tried and tested' person-centred values of humanistic counselling, baptised with healthy doses of liberal Western theology, become the underlying premises upon which the practice of universal pastoral counselling is based. Second, it at best denies and at worst suppresses cultural expressions that do not appear to conform to this mould. Difference is equated to deviance and is denied, suppressed or forced into conformity. An example of this would be any form of counselling that appears directive. Such would be seen as inappropriate, oppressive or outdated. Practitioners of such abominable arts as 'advising' or 'informing' are shunned or else offered courses in counselling skills.

Pastoral counselling in a mono-culturalist framework has tended to take the form of an insistence upon privacy, intimacy, confidentiality and surrogacy. Such counselling usually takes place in one-to-one sessions held in the privacy of the 'pastor's office'. It is premised upon the ability of clients and counsellors to self-disclose and to be articulate, autonomous, independent and self-directing – the predominant values of secular Western society. The point is that these values are assumed to be normative in all 'civilised societies'.

While pastoral counselling as described is of value for many in Western society, it must not be assumed to be so for all in multi-cultural societies in the West. The next approach to be described takes cultural difference more seriously.

Cross-culturalism

Basic maxim: 'They are totally (and pitifully) different from us.'
Pluralism is the credo of the cross-culturalist. Cross-cultural work in counselling has been based on cross-cultural psychology. The latter sought, from its inception in the 1960s and early 1970s, to study and respond to cultural variations in behaviour in a bid to validate or replicate generalisations about human behaviour based on white European or American studies. Studies undertaken in Europe or America were suitably modified and then undertaken in other parts of the world in order to ascertain the extent to which these generalisations were valid.

Cross-culturalists recognise cultural difference. Such difference is located in social groups which are constituted on the bases of identifiable physical, geographical or cultural characteristics. There are three sets of ideas that seem to be uppermost in the thinking of those who take this approach to the multi-cultural reality. First, the very fact of *difference* – namely, the recognition that real difference exists between groups of people in a society; that we are not all the same. Second, the view that the *boundaries* around groups are *fixed*, unalterable and, to a degree, impenetrable. Third, that each group has an *identity* which is shared by all who belong to the group. Identity is viewed as a bond that associates all who share it. It ties members together in a collective unity of homogeneity. Every member so identified is like everyone else within the social bond.

One of the pioneers of cross-cultural pastoral counselling is the American Mennonite David Augsburger. In a very useful book entitled *Pastoral Counseling across Cultures* (Augsburger 1986) he argues for the need for 'culturally capable pastoral counselors' who have the 'ability to join another in his or her culture while fully owning one's own' (1986: 19). Augsburger's aim is to assist in training culturally able counsellors who are at home on the boundary, able to cross over effectively into another culture with deep 'inter-pathic' understanding and then return to their own. Howard Clinebell, in the foreword to the book, captures this vision clearly:

> Crossing over to another culture with openness and reverence and then coming back is the spiritual adventure of our time, according to David Augsburger. In his view, crossing over with this mind-set and heart-set enables one to return to one's own culture enriched, more aware, more humble, and more alive. In a real sense, the power of this book is that it can enable us as readers to cross over, experience a stunning array of diverse cultural realities, and then return home with the treasure and growth-in-personhood that comes from interpathic caring in different worlds.
>
> (Augsburger 1986: 10)

Augsburger offers much that is of value and use in the encounter across cultures. However, there is a fundamental problem which emerges when one adopts this mentality. The difficulty is that it encourages a 'them' and 'us' mentality which creates problems in any pluralistic society. It is *we* (invariably the dominant, white European/American) who cross over to *them* (the 'rest') and then return. We do things to them. *We* learn about them. *They* are different from *us*. The unconscious assumption is that the counsellor belongs to the dominant majority and the client/patient to the other. The problem is highlighted for me as a black African pastoral counsellor in Britain – am I part of the 'we' or the 'them' on such reckoning?

Moodley and Dhingra (1998) have recently commented usefully on the complexity of the relationship between counsellor and client when the counsellor is of ethnic minority extraction. Bearing in mind McLeod's (1993) reminder that counselling remains a predominantly white occupation with relatively few ethnic minority counsellors, they explore the client's choice of counsellor. 'For white clients the appearance of a black counsellor may unconsciously evoke certain prejudices and stereotypes which could lead to the rejection of the counsellor but be interpreted by the client as not having a right to choose' (Moodley and Dhingra 1998: 296). They examine white clients' strategies in accepting black counsellors and black counsellors' strategies in managing the relationship. By exploring the questions of 'race' in therapy and facing up creatively to issues of difference, perception and expectation, they argue that white client and black counsellor 'can develop a rich environment for effective and creative therapeutic outcomes' (1998: 299).

A very real danger in the cross-cultural approach is the encouragement of division through the *essentialising* of cultural difference. Essentialising occurs when we make particular characteristics the only true or real expressions of a people. The assumption is that there exists an *authentic* African, Asian, African-Caribbean or black other who is totally different from the dominant one's own cultural experience. The 'exotic' other only exists in the imagination and fantasy of the person within the dominant culture. This way of thinking leads to stereotyping and is related to the overemphasis of cultural difference. It fails to recognise the mutual influence of cultures within multi-cultural societies. Moreover, it does not realise that cultural similarity may exist across cultural divisions.

In terms of pastoral care, the identity and difference of the 'other' is recognised as sacred and advocated for by carers and counsellors from the dominant culture. These brave souls become the 'experts' on 'the Asian community' or the 'black community'. They then become spokespersons for these cultural groups and inform the rest of the dominant group, relieving them of any responsibility to get involved themselves in the difficult business of cross-cultural encounter. In one sense these cultural informants vicariously bear the vulnerabilities of members of the dominant culture, who leave them to get on with it. Groups or committees are often formed to deal with ethnic minority concerns. The members of these groups are then the only ones who really make attempts to come to grips with the beliefs and practices of the 'others'. From time to time, members of the subaltern groups who successfully manage to cross over in the other direction become incorporated as token representatives of their cultures and evidence of the liberalism, kindness and tolerance of the dominant group.

Cross-culturalism represents a serious and valuable critique of mono-culturalism's presumption of universal values. Nevertheless, it operates on the basis of a flawed overemphasis on the identity, difference and homogeneity of other cultural or ethnic groups. While cross-culturalism overemphasises difference, educational multi-culturalism, which we will now discuss, oversimplifies cultural difference for the purposes of quick and easy encounter.

Educational multi-culturalism

Basic maxim: 'Aren't they interesting? We need to learn as much as we can about them.'
The fundamental premise upon which this approach is based is the need for accurate and detailed information to provide the basis for relevant policy and social action. If appropriate services are to be provided within a multi-cultural society, it would make sense for the nature and needs of the various cultural groups to be properly understood. Healthy 'race relations' within any community must be based on knowledge and information about the groups constituting the community. The approach to the multi-cultural society favoured here is that of 'facts and figures' as providing the necessary tools for effective action. As such, an attempt is made to build profiles of the various ethnic communities in the society which seek to give information about, for example, social customs, religious rites, food habits, leisure activities, family patterns, gender roles, education and housing within each group.

In Britain of the 1990s, ethnic monitoring questionnaires represent, in a crude form, this approach to the multi-cultural society. This survey approach certainly goes some way in providing information. However, the information generated in such ways is too often understood in a reductionistic and individualised way. It thus becomes fuel for cultural, ethnic, religious or other forms of stereotyping. Stereotyping involves perceiving and treating any particular individual member of a cultural group as bearing the presumed characteristics of that group. Stereo-typing homogenises groups, creating expectations of sameness among all who are classified as belonging to a group. Some attempts at multi-cultural education for counsellors and pastoral carers, in an attempt at informing them about 'ethnic minority clients', perpetuate stereotypical myths concerning, for example, the angry, underachieving Caribbean male; the Asian young woman's oppressive cultural role; the aggressive Muslim; or the problems of the Asian extended family system.

Along with categorising often goes placing in hierarchical order. Cultural groups are tacitly or at times explicitly placed in order of preference or value on particular characteristics. In such rankings the social or cultural group to which the one classifying belongs usually comes out on top. Moreover, there is an accompanying presumption that particular cultures are fixed or in some sense static. Canadian philosopher Charles Taylor, with reference to women, colonial subjects and black people, argues that the images produced by such listings of characteristics have the power to induce self-depreciation within the groups so described. Concerning black people, Taylor (1994) writes:

> white society has for generations projected a demeaning image of them, which some of them have been unable to resist adopting. Their own self-depreciation, in this view, becomes one of the most potent instruments of their own oppression.
>
> (1994: 75)

Educational multi-culturalism adopts a commendable information-based, scientific data-oriented approach to the multi-cultural. However, like cross-culturalism, it fails to avoid stereotyping, reductionism, individualising, placing groups in hierarchical order and perpetuating myths that, when imbibed, can induce self-hatred within the sub-dominant groups. Educational multi-culturalism is often led by media, consumer, tourist, quick-fix or market considerations. Busy pastoral counsellors wish to be able to obtain rapidly the information they need to enable them to visit or counsel their ethnic minority clients. So they turn to these manuals of information as they would to tourist guides. The problem is the gross oversimplification of the cultural, which can mislead and distort any real human relationships to be found therein.

Pastoral counsellors who operate on such premises are often sensitive and caring persons who seek as much information as they can obtain in order not to offend or act inappropriately with the cultural other. However, what is lost in a dependence on this information is the spontaneity and sensitivity which is a *sine qua non* of genuine human interaction. 'For pastoral care to be real it has to arise in the midst of genuine human encounter where carer and cared for are both vulnerable and open' (Lartey 1998: 49).

Inter-culturality

Basic maxim: 'Every human person is in some respects (a) like all others (b) like some others (c) like no other.'

In order to gain a fuller understanding of human persons within the global community, it is necessary to explore the ways in which culture, individual uniqueness and human characteristics work together to influence persons. Kluckholn and Murray's (1948) phrase quoted above captures these three spheres of influence which act simultaneously in the experience of every human person. By 'human characteristics' (we are *like all others*), I refer to that which all humans as humans share. This includes physiological, cognitive and psychological capabilities, with all the common human variations in them. The 'cultural' (we are *like some others*) refers to characteristic ways of knowing, interpreting and valuing the world which we receive through the socialisation processes we go through in our social groupings. These include world-views, values, preferences and interpretative frames as well as language, customs and forms of social relationship. The 'individual' (like *no other*) or 'personal' indicates that there are characteristics – both physical (e.g. fingerprint and dental configuration) and psycho-social – which are unique to individuals.

These spheres of human experience interact constantly in living human persons who continually learn, grow and change. Inter-cultural pastoral counsellors seek to work with persons in the light of these presuppositions and realisations. In any pastoral counselling encounter three kinds of issues are attended to by the inter-cultural pastoral counsellor. First, there is an attempt to enquire what of the common experience we all share as human persons is to be found in the particular situation in question. The attempt here is in recognition and affirmation of the fact that all human beings are created in and reflect the image of God. The assumption, therefore, is that despite variations, ambiguities and differences there will be evidence of humanity in all pastoral counselling encounters. Second, there will be an attempt to figure out what in the experience being dealt with is the result of social and cultural forces: attention will need to be paid to specific socio-cultural views and practices relevant to the social group the counselling partner recognises as their own. What would need to be encouraged would be an affirmative as well as self-critical and open exploration of these cultural views and practices in an attempt to discover their influence upon the issue being examined. Within multi-cultural environments, the influence of other cultures than one's own will need to be investigated. Questions of power, domination, benefit and suffering are of particular poignancy here. Third, in intercultural pastoral counselling, attempts will be made to investigate what in the experience could be said to be uniquely attributable to the personal characteristics of the counselling partner.

In an approach that comes close to what is proposed here, Lago and Thompson (1996) argue that multi-culturally skilled counsellors develop identifiable characteristics. Within a format reminiscent of Egan's three-phase model of helping processes and following the work of Sue and Sue (1990), they propose three stages in the practice of such counsellors. These are, first, 'counsellor awareness of own assumptions, values and biases'; second, 'understanding the world-view of the culturally different client'; and finally, 'developing appropriate intervention strategies and techniques' (Lago and Thompson 1996: 136). The dimensions along which these develop are beliefs, attitudes, knowledge and skills. This helpfully provides us with a grid and a process to assist in the training of multi-culturally skilled counsellors, which, if used sensitively and not mechanically, can be of much use.

The pastoral counsellor who wishes to work in an inter-cultural manner has to attend carefully to the common humanity shared by all people. He or she needs to face up to their own vulnerability in an open and honest way. There needs to be a levelling in which counsellors and clients recognise each other as made in the image of God and reflecting that image in their humanity. Much in terms of recognition and respect, especially on the part of counsellors who belong to or participate in dominant and/or historically oppressive groups, of the other in their otherness, needs to be acknowledged. If there is to be any genuine human encounter, attempts need to be made to equalise the relationship through mutual awareness of power dynamics in such inter-cultural encounters.

Second, attention will need to be paid to differences and similarities that arise out of cultural factors. Here, knowledge and information about specific socio-cultural, historical, economic and political matters of relevance to the cultures represented in the counselling relationship may be valuable. But perhaps more germane to the process will be the exploration of the ways, as perceived especially by the client, in which culture has in the past exerted and continues to exert an influence on the experience or issue in question.

Third, questions will be faced as to what each person experiences uniquely. No matter how embedded one might be in one's social or cultural grouping, there will be characteristic ways in which one experiences or faces issues that will need addressing.

At various moments in any pastoral encounter one or other of these aspects of our humanity will be the focus of attention. Nevertheless, inter-cultural pastoral counselling will attempt always to have the other aspects in view and to hold all three in creative and dynamic tension. Here, a Christian trinitarian and communitarian vision might prove useful. As with the distinct Persons of the Trinity, so with the features of our human experience. They can be and often need to be viewed and treated on their own in order to be taken seriously and more carefully attended to. Time and effort, for example, need to be spent discussing and exploring the nature of the Person of Christ. Nevertheless, the relational character of the three Persons must never be entirely lost sight of. In a similar way, the 'human', the cultural and the personal in all human persons need to be attended to on their own while also being seen as in creative and dynamic interaction with each other.

REFERENCES

Augsburger, D.W. (1986) *Pastoral Counseling across Cultures*, Philadelphia: Westminster.

Berinyuu, A.A. (1989) *Towards Theory and Practice of Pastoral Counseling in Africa*, Frankfurt: Peter Lang.

Ghunney, J. (1993) 'Ghana', in R.J. Wicks and B.K. Estadt, (eds), *Pastoral Counseling in the Global Church*, Maryknoll, NY: Orbis, pp. 82–104.

Halmos, P. (1965) *Faith of the Counsellors*, London: Constable.

Kluckholn, C. and Murray, H. (1948) *Personality in Nature, Society and Culture*, New York: Alfred Knoff.

Lago, C. and Thompson, J. (1996) *Race, Culture and Counselling*, Buckingham: Open University Press.

Lambourne, R.A. (1974) 'Religion, medicine and politics', *Contact*, 44: 1–40.

Lartey, E.Y. (1993) 'African perspectives on pastoral theology', *Contact*, 112: 3–12.

—— (1997) *In Living Colour: An Intercultural Approach to Pastoral Care and Counselling*, London: Cassell.

—— (1998) 'The Fernley Hartley Lecture. Pastoral care in multi-cultural Britain: white, black or beige?' *Epworth Review*, 25(3): 42–52.

Masamba ma Mpolo and Nwachuku, D. (eds) (1991) *Pastoral Care and Counselling in Africa Today*, Frankfurt/M: Peter Lang.

Maynard, A. (1998) 'Beginning at the beginning, Islamic counselling', *Race Multi-Cultural Journal*, 16: 22–24.

McLeod, J. (1993) *An Introduction to Counselling*, Buckingham: Open University Press.

Moodley, R. and Dhingra, S. (1998) 'Cross-cultural/racial matching in counselling and therapy: white clients and black counsellors', *Counselling*, 9(4): 295–9.

Mulrain, G. (1995) 'Bereavement counselling among African Caribbean people in Britain', *Contact*, 118: 9–14.

Sue, D.W and Sue, D. (1990) *Counseling the Culturally Different*, New York: Wiley.

Taylor, C. (1994) 'The politics of recognition', in D.T. Goldberg (ed.), *Multiculturalism: A Critical Reader*, Oxford: Blackwell.

Wicks, R.J. and Estadt, B.K. (eds) (1993) *Pastoral Counseling in a Global Church: Voices from the Field*, Maryknoll, NY: Orbis.

Wilson, M.J. (1988) *A Coat of Many Colours*, London: Epworth.

3

THE PLACE OF RELIGIOUS TRADITION IN PASTORAL COUNSELLING

Alistair Ross

Introduction

The last Saturday before Christmas an irate shopper bawled at me (after I had offered her an invitation to a church service), 'It's all this religion that spoils Christmas.' The word 'religion' evokes strongly negative responses in many people who have no sense that it can be captivatingly enriching, contribute to wholeness of being, and bring about salvation. What people want, it seems, is to be holistic with no notion of holiness. If you add the word 'tradition' to 'religion' you get a very different reaction. The words evoke a wide range of sensory experiences: church bells; country parsons; graveyards; incense; damp, musty smells; archaic quaintness with an Agatha Christie quality; a way of life that time forgot; hymns no longer sung in assemblies; the mischievous innocence of choirboys; priests remote from sexuality and the world; black clothed, bearded, skull-capped Jewish men swaying in prayer before a wall – so the many images continue to spill over in an other-worldly anachronistic collage.

Religious tradition has, in the words of a highly successful advertising guru, John Hegharty, 'an image problem'. The advertising world does not advertise a failing product with a snappy caption. All that will do is highlight the problem. They go back to basics to discover what made it successful in the past and discover ways in which it can be successful again. One area in which religious tradition is deemed to have a major image problem is the relatively new world of psychiatry, psychology, psychoanalysis, psychotherapy and counselling. Influenced by Nietzsche's illusion that God was dead, Freud's performance of the last rites was at one level premature, yet it was also powerfully significant. With the knowledge that God was terminally ill the psychiatrist and psychoanalyst became the new priests – the inheritors and interpreters of the psyche of a godless society. Religious tradition was seen as the redundant heritage of an illusory Father figure (Wulff 1991; Ward 1993).

Yet there is the clear expectation from many that religious beliefs and values need to be addressed as part of the counselling process. Take the case of Jitendra (whose story is explored by six different therapeutic approaches). Jitendra is an Indian psychiatrist in his early forties. Born in Uganda, he was brought up with a Hindu background and he later came to Britain where he married a woman from an Irish Protestant background. This has resulted in

> personal conflict and suffering, I would say, directly with my wife, and indirectly in relation to the children, and what one should tell them about how one should view the world . . . I think there is a thing beyond it, and that is to do with . . . it is a deeper question of meaning, enlightenment or salvation. . . . And I would expect a therapist to perhaps tackle that at some stage. I would expect that sort of interaction. If it wasn't it would be terrible . . . it would be a gap in the relationship for me.
>
> (Jacobs 1996: 10–11)

However, there has been a move which in some ways appears healthy, but which in fact maintains a 'split' between religious tradition and counselling. This is the growing awareness and acceptance of spirituality – but in a way which divorces it from religion. Religious tradition is seen as dogma, whereas spirituality is seen as a universal free spirit of discovery related to meanings and values. Such a spirituality becomes a pantheistic embracing of anything and everything and is as elusive as the famous Loch Ness monster. I have the T-shirt, the mug, the poster and the photograph but no real evidence of the actual thing. This type of spirituality appeals to our consumer-shaped unconscious – what we choose to buy is shaped as much by the packaging as by the content. Yet so often it is divorced from religious traditions, giving the form of faith without the substance. It is in this hostile amphitheatre among the lions that pastoral counselling finds itself.

The call and challenge to the Church to go 'back to basics' applies in the area of pastoral counselling. I define pastoral counselling (though other definitions are offered in this book) as a relationship in which a person agrees to explore issues of meaning and being, helped by another, drawing on psychological and spiritual insights informed by a tradition shaped within a community of faith. But what are these traditions? What does it mean to go 'back to basics'? Pastoral counselling has deep subterranean roots stretching down to the origins of religious faith and to the depths of personal being. Tom Oden, an American theologian, prophetically challenged pastoral carers and counsellors to return to their roots at an international conference in Edinburgh in 1979. Oden shared his concern that the Church had abandoned its rich heritage of pastoral care for therapeutic insights, and in so doing had lost its distinctive identity. Writing of Gregory the Great's (AD 540–604) *Book of Pastoral Rule*, Oden (1984) demonstrates how it anticipated much of what is found in contemporary theories without losing touch with the witness of religious tradition. Thus, Oden takes us back to the Church Fathers. Frank Lake, a missionary, psychiatrist and pastoral theologian, reaches back further to the Gospel accounts of Jesus, especially John's. In *Clinical Theology* (Lake 1966), the dominant paradigm was the psychological, theological and normative human pattern of the life of Jesus, which Lake termed the 'dynamic cycle'. Jesus is the ultimate demonstration of authentic personhood and, by inference, the unique exponent of pastoral counselling. Jesus followed in a rich rabbinic tradition of wise teachers who surveyed the whole of life and saw it rooted in the religious traditions of family, community, ceremony, symbol, worship and the revealing of God. The story of Job describes the counsel of Job's three friends, perplexed but willing to wait until he was ready to explore the traumas of his experience. Jewish tradition also draws on the Mishnah, the Talmud, Midrash and other codes and writings to enlarge and reveal the ways in which God is known.

Pastoral counselling not only has deep roots but widespread roots, like a strawberry plant, that cover a vast area encompassing different religious traditions. I rediscovered this when I was part of a multi-faith working party developing a National Vocational Qualification in pastoral counselling. The group convenor had anticipated that there would be difficulties in getting us to agree a common set of values when in fact this was the easiest and most enjoyable part of working together. We did recognise that every religious tradition had strands within it that were dogmatic and exclusive, yet we were able to find some common values that related to pastoral counselling. Where we disagreed was over our psychological and therapeutic theories. Whilst I valued this multi-faith exploration of pastoral counselling with the abundance of wise sayings and insights such religions offer, it is only in more recent times that these have been applied to pastoral counselling. I write, then, from within my own tradition of Christianity and another monotheistic tradition, Judaism, with their long traditions of pastoral dealings with people. These are offered as an enriching dimension to any multi-faith discussion of pastoral counselling that does proper justice to their heritage.

So what is at the core of these religious traditions? What strands weave these monotheistic religions together? Is there a bedrock of ideas related to pastoral care and counselling that can be rediscovered and reapplied in today's world, rather than remaining dormant like some fossilised ideology? I would like to suggest that there are four key areas of religious tradition that can find expression in pastoral counselling and each of these is linked to the other. Everyone has a belief system of some sort or another and there are times when the value and the strength of these beliefs are threatened and questioned (Jacobs 1993). We seek an answer or a solution. We access that religious dimension of our being that enables us to ask questions of meaning in relation to our experience. We are enabled to answer these questions in the context of pastoral counselling through the experience of revelation which is made possible by the pastoral counselling relationship, especially one in which questions of morality and ultimate values can be explored. These answers, or the ability to ask the question and accept that there is not always an answer, can become a source of hope and salvation to us.

The question 'Why?'

'Why', said the four-year-old boy standing with his blue bucket and spade, exploring the exciting seaside world of which he is becoming increasingly aware, 'does the sea come in and go away?' Eventually, the adult descends to the ultimate answer to a 'why?' question, 'Because I say so.' At this, the boy gives up and goes about building his sandcastle. The question 'why?' is a vital philosophical and religious question, which we in the late twentieth century are beginning to ask again (Scruton 1996). For much of this century, the entire focus in thinking and enquiry has been on 'how?'. If something is self-explanatory or can be understood in terms of itself or as part of a closed system, then the question 'why?' makes no sense. 'Why did my husband die?', asks a distraught and sobbing thirty-year-old woman, hearing the tragic news of a road accident. Such an event can be explained in terms of forces, chemistry and biology. A motorist under the influence of alcohol miscalculated his speed and hit another car in a head-on collision, the combined force of which propelled the husband through the windscreen despite the restraint of a seat-belt, causing severe trauma to the skull which was unable to protect the brain, the trauma to which resulted in death. No one would be heartless enough to put it precisely in those terms but that is the explanation in terms of 'how' and 'cause and effect'. 'Why?' is another aspect, and this century dominated by a scientific paradigm has tended to neglect it until confronted by the Holocaust (Cohen-Brook 1996) and other such dreadful events. Kenneth Wilson, a religious philosopher, sees 'Why? as the fundamental question about me and the fact that I, or the universe, exist at all' (personal communication), and the question 'why?' is never more important than when we confront the reality of death. 'Why' wants to know about meaning rather than mechanics. 'Why?' is a frequent refrain in the Bible and in other religious writing, perhaps summed up in Rabbi Harold Kushner's (1989) book *When Bad Things Happen to Good People*.

Whilst our religious traditions allow us to question, these need addressing, and it is often done through a restating of the traditional answers of a particular faith community. However, for many this is not enough and they want a place or a relationship where they can explore these questions in relation to their own lives. Pastoral counselling is such a place and provides such a relationship because it becomes the place of fresh understanding and revelation where we see things in a new way. 'Why does God allow it?'; 'What does God care?'; 'No wonder nobody believes nowadays', are all comments made to me in counselling. Pastoral counselling draws on a religious context that says these questions matter profoundly – as evidenced in the wrestling of Job, the abandonment of the Psalmist, the betrayal of Jesus in Gethsemane followed by his agonising death at Golgotha, the countless unnamed martyrs throughout the centuries, culminating in our own with the experience of the Jewish people in the unparalleled horrors of the Holocaust (Bloomfield 1997). Yet those experiences of evil and suffering are 'out there'. Pastoral counselling brings into the counselling arena those awful questions which probe at the depths of our being and expose the depth of our faith. 'Where was God when that man, I cannot call him father, tied me down and raped me?' The wounds of many people with so much faith are as deep as if in some bottomless, dark chasm. Lake, as a pastoral theologian, believed and wrote that it was in this abyss, in the near disintegration of their being, that people encountered God, who in Christ had been there and was there to take them home towards wholeness and holiness. The start of this journey is in the revelatory activity that is a vital part of pastoral counselling and to which we now turn.

Revelation and experiencing the transpersonal

Revelation describes a process or event by which God (described in male and female terms but not limited by these gender distinctions) makes himself known. Such revelation influences the life of a person, leading to a new awareness of the transpersonal dimension of being, a new experience, expression or commitment to religious faith, values and traditions. Revelation comes in many forms – for example, the glory of God experienced by Moses at Mount Sinai which resulted in the giving of the law, the Torah. It is present in the sense that we are not alone, since the creation points to one who is beyond us so that the 'why' question becomes the 'who' question. It is also present in the dynamic activity of God described in the Orthodox tradition in Trinitarian terms or in the Catholic and Protestant traditions in terms of special revelation focused on Jesus Christ. Much contemporary theology is more focused on the experiential, the existential and progressive views of God speaking here and now, whilst also seeing God unveiling himself through history and the narrative of people's experience. Without revelation there would be no religion and no pastoral counselling. How do these ideas fit together? Revelation, as the word itself suggests, reveals aspects of God that are unknown by any other process and which result in an active 'knowing'. Revelation changes people through knowledge, encounter and a retrospective sharing in the earlier encounters of others through the expression of faith. So, revelation is both an objective event and a subjective experience, and the balance is held by the recognition of both of these objective and subjective elements. Different religious traditions focus on one rather than the other. An evangelical Christian would focus on the 'objective' expressed in Scripture but focused especially on Jesus Christ, experienced in salvation. A liberal Jew would focus on making sense of the world now in the light of the traditions of faith passed faithfully on from generation to generation through a special 'chosen' people. Unlike orthodox Judaism, this is a progressive revelation in which each person and each community participates now. Much revelation in religious traditions comes through texts which are believed to enshrine the very word of God.

Pastoral counselling is a similarly revelatory activity in a subjective sense, and it also can provides new insights into the objective nature of revelation. People become aware of themselves through the agency of another in a way that is experienced as new and revelatory, which broadens the nature of theological exploration to include not just traditional religious texts but also the text of the person's life. Depending on one's view this life can be either a discovery of general truths about life and God (which stops short of an actual encounter with God), or an actual revelatory discovery of God, the source Being, in our own experience of being, through a counselling relationship which explores the question of being. The pastoral counsellor is part of a wider faith tradition that helps each person tell their story in a faith context as well as within their personal context. This is clearly seen in the tension many Christians feel in relationship to God as Father. So many people (though not all) have grown up under the tyranny of domineering fathers that even reciting the Lord's Prayer causes pain to emerge once again. The vision of a heavenly father is obscured by the scars contained within and the memories that cannot be erased. When this convergence is experienced in worship that has historically been dominated by a patriarchal world-view, the consequence is often to leave people with unresolved feelings of worthlessness as the internal and the external worlds of faith, feeling, memory and emotion collide. Pastoral counselling holds the tension of a Christian and propositional understanding of revelation or a Torah and interpretation understanding of revelation in contrast with a more contemporary, transpersonal narrative revealing of being. The forces are often unequal and threaten to distort, if not destroy, what is held in place, like the forces at work in an atom holding the potentially explosive power in creative tension. The counsellor contains or holds the person experiencing the tensions, the confusions, the hurts, the 'why?' questions, the moral agonising and in doing so becomes a bridge, a mediator, an interpreter or translator for the questions that the client brings. As they face questions, feelings, emotions and memories, clients can experience a more genuine revelation of God, unhindered by the overwhelming force of personal narrative. Pastoral counselling offered in the context of a faith tradition does provide the space for a genuinely new or deeper understanding of God and oneself.

The value of relationship

What makes pastoral counselling an arena for experiencing the transpersonal encountered in revelation is the personal, the dimension of relationship. The pastoral counselling relationship provides an arena or a 'transitional space' (Abram 1996: 326) in which some revelatory understanding of experience can be developed. The reason for this lies in our being created for relationship, which Christians see as an expression of the Trinitarian being of God who has always existed in relationship. All that God creates in people or cosmos is in relationship and through it God acts providentially in our lives. We see this reflected in the ravenous appetite in each person for relationship, and the purpose of revelation is to show us how relationship with God and others comes about. For the Christian tradition the focus is on Jesus Christ. In the person of Jesus we see the perfect dynamic cycle which Lake used as a pattern for all normal development. He also used it as a diagnostic tool for interpreting how aspects of being had gone wrong. Whilst Lake adapted much object-relations theory in his development of the dynamic cycle, his theological foundation was Jesus as the perfect revelation of what it was to be fully human, as God had intended us to be. Each human being seeks relationship (initially perceived as an object) from the moment of birth, yet that relationship has already begun before birth. One of the fascinating features of recent work done on lone twins whose twin died before birth is how significant as adults they perceive this relationship to be (Woodward 1998).

This psychological aspect of being – the need for relationship – finds a theological explanation in our being made for relationship with God. All other relationships are but constellations around this sun. This relationship with God is affirmed in all religious traditions. It is a destiny all share, whether faith is acknowledged or not. Our lives may not be what they were destined to be but within them are signposts to transcendence. In pastoral counselling those signposts are read by the person learning to risk asking questions as well as looking for answers. The process of transmission is difficult to quantify. Some see it as an unconscious process, others as coincidence, others as the work of the Spirit and a few as a combination of all of them.

At a recent conference on the subject of counselling in education I saw someone in the hundred-strong audience I was sure I recognised but could not put a name to. In the break I confidently went up to them only to discover Gill had never met or seen me before. This triggered an intriguing conversation where it became clear that we had a religious faith in common. In later correspondence Gill recognised that she was 'at sea' spiritually and when I had offered to explore the relationship between faith and therapy, this had been of great significance to her, so much so that she interpreted our meeting as far from accidental. How can I explain this? As a person of faith, I see a spiritual, transcendent dimension to all being (not just pastoral counselling) which communicates; and I believe that a great deal of the Spirit's work is with the unconscious as a person engages in relationship with other people. The sheer relationality of people, both our need for it and the genuine difficulties we encounter in it, overwhelms me.

Pastoral counselling provides a relational context that allows these many-stranded, unconscious, narrative-influenced, spiritual and godward dimensions to emerge. Once a relationship of trust has been established

– a major therapeutic task in its own right – the places where religious tradition results in conflict (the nature of being, the place of authority, the taking of responsibility, or the conditional nature of love, acceptance and forgiveness, the exploration of diversity and paradox in oneself and in one's experience of God) can be explored. All this can be found in a pastoral counselling relationship that allows space for a new reflection and revealing drawn from our faith tradition.

The pastoral counselling relationship can also draw on the rich heritage of symbolism found in all religious traditions. There is an immense power to be found in the imagination as one engages with a text, such as the Bible, as it becomes symbolic of a spiritual dimension. Inhabitants of the Radio 4 mythical 'Desert Island' are still given a Bible, even in these secular days. Such power is also found in the awareness of the senses in contemplation of an icon or other forms of religious art as a means of transcendent reality that transforms the senses. There is also an immensity about participation in a ritual or a ceremony that stretches back thousands of years and is shared by other believers at the same time throughout the world. Survivors of the Holocaust recall the symbolic value of prayer as a statement of hope in the malevolent despair of darkness and evil so common in such death camps. Daily prayer linked the Jewish people to their ancestors who had suffered and survived before. Pastoral counselling draws on these symbolic functions found in many religious traditions. The counsellor becomes a companion, like the friends who sat in mourning and grief with Job, helping to interpret the belief of those around and of Job himself. Yet, ultimately all they could do was form the context in which Job was able to make his own discovery of faith in God for himself. The pastoral counsellor can also become a sign or symbol of hope, a representation of normality, a proof of order, a personification of connection, and a token of the meaning carried by symbols within religious traditions. An example is bread and wine in the Protestant service of communion, which are taken until Jesus returns as a symbol of hope. They incorporate the Christian into relationship with God. They are token of life and death, sin, failure and forgiveness. They bring about a new order, a new way of being that characterises all of life. They symbolise the past, the present and the future. Powerful symbols, for some they actually become the body and blood of Jesus Christ. It would be at best arrogant, and at worst blasphemous, to say that pastoral counsellors become Jesus Christ and do what Christians claim Jesus did. Yet they are powerfully symbolic, and much more so for people of strong belief. Some evidence of that is found in the enormous complexities of being both a counsellor and a priest to the extent that I will not see people for pastoral counselling with whom I have another pastoral relationship as their minister, except in crisis intervention situations. Even this may communicate a view that God is only interested in crises and then goes away again. This takes us on to the area of hope and salvation.

Hope, love and salvation

Every religious faith offers hope, love and salvation. It comes in many different ways, and the adherents of each faith tradition have shed blood over the rightness of their views. People need salvation today, long for love and desire hope. Such these themes are found throughout contemporary culture, where people like the pop music icons Madonna and Eric Clapton (according to lyrics on their most recent CDs) want their sins to be dealt with. Counselling is not totally equipped to help in all these areas; at best it can save us from some aspects of ourselves or offer an unconditional acceptance that is the closest experience to love that many people experience but it cannot offer what people want in terms of faith. Pastoral counselling recognises these faith issues and offers a way of exploring the human need for redemption, for sin to be paid for, atoned. Pastoral counselling does touch on forgiveness, reconciliation, fear and hope, love, yet is self-aware enough not to offer salvation. Pastoral counselling dares to believe that the revelation of salvation in a faith sense needs the revelation of a loving relationship that both allows a questioning and offers hope. Robinson (1998) explores this further in his article 'Helping the hopeless: exploring love as the ground of what is hoped for'.

In our supposedly secular age, pastoral counselling takes the values of religious traditions and gives to people a moral and spiritual voice once more. It reminds people that the great religious themes of the past are still with us. They may not be marketed well or come with glossy packaging or even be advertised attractively by the people who profess faith. Yet, as we head into a new millennium there is hope and there is salvation, and pastoral counselling stands as a bridge between the world of the spiritual and the world of the psychological.

Louise: a case study

How does this work in practice? In the following case study we shall see how strands of these vital aspects of religious tradition weave in and out of a personal narrative explored in pastoral counselling. At times they are clearly seen, like the view from a Swiss mountain, yet they can also become as elusive as the mist-shrouded descent of Ben Nevis.

Louise came to me for counselling, knowing that I was also a minister and the bearer of a faith tradition – a part of me which she experienced in counselling. The story began when I was invited into her family home (her mother and sister had started to attend church) to spend some time with her brother, grieving at the death of his best friend. The raw emotions of sudden death by misadventure, the oppressive feelings of guilt, the stagnant presence of loss and the unanaesthetised pain had gathered like vultures at an unexpected feast. Into this emotion-choked room I came as a trusted outsider, trusted because of my role as a minister and my personal faith as a Christian. I was a bearer of a religious tradition that did hold values, morality, standards but these are enshrined in the person. Louise could see in me the priest and the therapist. Louise was in the background and whatever I did that day as I listened and stayed with the agony, not promising easy or glib answers, made an impact on her like a seed sown in fertile soil.

Louise rang me several months later saying with characteristic bluntness that her life was in a mess and it needed sorting out, asking to come to see me. At first she seemed out to shock, to push boundaries (complaining, for example, that she could not smoke). A long, tangled story emerged, a story of someone desperately looking for intimacy, who expressed her search through casual sexual encounters because Louise could control a low-risk intimacy that demanded little of her. Louise would not let anyone close but slowly began to trust me and allow me to see the 'real' her because I was 'one of the good guys.' Part of the testing was to see how I would cope with her sexual lifestyle, so different from that of my faith tradition. Louise's behaviour and lifestyle were clearly at odds with my religious tradition of monogamous marriage, yet I made no criticism, expressing only concern. The journey and companionship allowed space for the real Louise to emerge, a frightened girl with needs and longings, who was out of her depth in an adult world but adept at her survival within it. One session Louise announced, 'I haven't slept with anyone for a month; aren't you proud of me?' Here was Louise telling me that she had made moral progress even though that had not been a part of our contract in counselling. It does raise the question, however, of how free can clergy be from their role in pastoral counselling and this is an area that will inevitably lead to confusion and tension. How will I respond when Louise does something that I perceive to be wrong objectively and psychologically? These were some of the questions Louise raised in her week by week encounter. Yet this revelation for her was a new chapter for Louise; I had never suggested this to her but we explored how feeling good was not something that others could give to her – she needed to begin to value herself. We looked back to a previous relationship where her partner died, and she asked 'why?'. Those questions haunted her but as she asked them in the context of a relationship, Louise began to see how her use of her sexuality was her expression of anger at men who always let her down, even dying on her. I suggested that ultimately I would let her down too (I knew at that stage that I would be moving within the next year). She began to explore the parts of her that were being revealed in counselling. Some she liked and others she didn't, but Louise came to build a more complete picture of herself.

We still needed to explore another issue, which I knew to be why, at one level, Louise was seeing me as a counsellor: I was still a religious authority figure with all the projections that people bring to that role. Slowly, it emerged that in Louise's experience of counselling there was a sacramental element; she was looking for a place to confess and to receive absolution. As she said, 'It's a bit like going to confession, you do feel good afterwards.' Through pastoral counselling Louise saw she was seeking absolution from a great deal more than a list of sexual sins. Such absolution was never formally asked for or given but it was an important undercurrent to the already complex dynamics, and the counselling would have been less rich had this not been owned and explored.

Louise did come to value herself much more and see herself and her behaviour in another light. There were moments of transcendent encounter and realisation, and whilst this is not the same as salvation, such signals of transcendence arising in and through a counselling relationship point us beyond, so that Louise announced one day, 'You know, there might even be a God after all.' Hope, which I believe to be a vital contribution of pastoral counselling to the broader counselling world, began to emerge in Louise's life. She came to a point of making a commitment in a relationship that was to be permanent and based on more than just sex. This in itself did not guarantee a happy ending, and the relationship did finish; but Louise was not destroyed by this as she had once feared. She found space in her life for the new aspects of herself that she had worked so hard to recover and accept. Her spiritual needs were still unresolved, despite her subsequent occasional church attendance, but they had at least been uncovered and valued. Louise said of herself that she could never be the same person again. That for me is a testimony to hope and a movement in a better direction.

Summary

The four themes explored here that underpin many religious traditions across a range of understandings are: the 'space' to ask vital questions about meaning in relation to our experience; discovering the revelation of God belongs not only 'out there' but 'in here' through human experience; the expression of this in a particular pastoral counselling relationship; and the holding out of a hand of love to the future in terms of hope and salvation. They have been part of the pastoral tradition of care held by the Church and other religious communities down through the centuries. Sadly, the life of religious traditions has another dimension which at times has worked against these life-affirming principles. The Church, to take one example, has become the prohibitor, the rule-enforcer, the boundary keeper and the withholder. In themselves these are not necessarily wrong. Contemporary postmodern society has developed a profoundly disturbing eclecticism that leaves people as trapped in their micro-narratives as the reviled meta-narrative of faith. By recognising the value and the danger of religious tradition, pastoral counselling has something to offer. The values we have explored here, the dangers of religious leaders becoming controlling figures and part of patriarchal and patronising leadership infused with power, are still very real – but a fuller exploration lies elsewhere in this book. Religious faith, whatever tradition it represents, if it is true faith, is about trust and growth. Neither of these is ever free from pain or risk. The risk is that if people are enabled to experience life and faith for themselves in the rawness and flawedness of our contemporary world, they may not return with quite the same faith they had before. Yet, faith is about letting people return when they can and Jesus has some vital and contemporary words to say about the waiting, hurting father, the self-righteous but angry brother and the more integrated prodigal son (Luke 15: 11–32). Pastoral counsellors need to attend to the vital place and role of religious tradition in a counselling world that has overlooked this. A part of any counselling is to attend to the transpersonal needs of clients and for some time clients have been short-changed. Even though spirituality is back on many counsellors' agenda there still needs to be further recognition that in itself this is not sufficient. The quasi-religious dimension of counselling, given that it can be such a revelatory activity, needs to look again to religious traditions that allow and encourage those questions that touch at the deepest human and religious need – to be in relationship not just with oneself, or others, but with God.

REFERENCES

Abram, J. (1996) *The Language of WINNICOTT*, London, Karnac.
Bloomfield, I. (1997) 'Counselling Holocaust survivors', *Counselling*, 8(1): 42–7.
Cohen-Brook, D. (1996) *God and the Holocaust*, Leominster: Gracewing.
Jacobs, M. (1993) *Still Small Voice* (2nd edn), London: SPCK.
—— (ed.) (1996) *Jitendra – Lost Connections*, Buckingham: Open University Press.
Kushner, H. (1989) *When Bad Things Happen to Good People*, New York: Schocken.
Lake, F. (1966) *Clinical Theology*, London: DLT.
Lyall, D. (1997) *Pastoral Care in a Postmodern Context*, Oxford: Clinical Theology Association.
Oden, T. (1984) *Care of Souls in the Classic Tradition*, Philadelphia: Fortress.
Robinson, S. (1998) 'Helping the hopeless: exploring love as the ground of what is hoped for', *Contact*, 127: 3–10.
Scruton, R. (1996) *An Intelligent Person's Guide to Philosophy*, London: Duckworth.
Ward, I. (ed.) (1993) *Is Psychoanalysis Another Religion?*, London: Freud Museum.
Wilson, K. (1998) (Personal communication 29 September 1998).
Woodward, J. (1998) *The Lone Twin: Understanding Twin Bereavement and Loss*, London: Free Association Books.
Wulff, D. (1991) *Psychology of Religion: Classic and Contemporary Views*, New York: Wiley.

4

PASTORAL COUNSELLING
AND PRAYER

Jessica Rose

Introduction

A Russian friend of mine was looking through some books when
he came across a title which mystified him. It was Ellenberger's history
of psychoanalysis, *The Discovery of the Unconscious* (1970). What on
earth, he wondered, could such a book be about? It was not that he had
not heard of psychoanalysis nor understood some of its basic precepts.
What amazed him was that anyone could think of the unconscious as
a recent discovery. For him, it was simply a fact of life experienced,
often painfully, through his interactions with others, and in prayer and
the sacraments, but above all as a mystery which had been exercising
consciousness ever since we began as human beings to think about
ourselves and our condition.

This is a perspective which pastoral counselling needs to reclaim.
Psychological thinking and practice has had such an enormous influence
that it is easy to assume that pastoral counselling is a product of modern
psychology, forgetting that it has existed ever since there have been
religious traditions within which people seek to help each other. In any
religious enterprise prayer plays a central part which tends to be lost
when the focus becomes psychological, a point which is made particularly strongly by Tom Oden (Oden 1984). At the same time it is
important to bear in mind that all three major psychological movements,
the psychoanalytic, cognitive-behavioural and humanist-existentialist,
have criticised religious systems for failing to address people where
they were. They have flourished and taken root precisely because they
were right in this. The questions which arise through the practice of
prayer within the counselling relationship demonstrate both the value of

psychological awareness in human relationships and its limitations. This exploration of the place of prayer in counselling will draw on the Orthodox Christian tradition with which I am most at home. Many of its basic concepts, however, will be familiar to those who practise prayer within other faith traditions.

Working with prayer in the pastoral counselling relationship

The intimate encounter between a pastoral counsellor and someone who has come for help has implications not only for the persons concerned and those closest to them, but for the faith community as a whole. It is perhaps easy to see how prayer embraces all of these aspects. For the religious person (and this will usually apply to both counsellor and client in a pastoral context) prayer is not an added extra: it is, as William James called it, 'the very soul and essence of religion' (James 1902/1982: 464). Thus, from the beginning the relationship may involve the prayer of both parties and that of the praying communities to which they belong, whether or not these are explicitly discussed. In addition, it may well be that sessions begin or end with prayer, that prayer is talked about, and help given with how to pray or how to understand prayer. Between sessions, the work may well affect and be affected by the prayer of client and counsellor. Many pastoral counsellors take the people they work with specifically into their own prayer, and pray regularly for themselves and their work, committing it to God.

Working specifically with prayer may include asking how a person prays, what they believe about prayer and so on. This is no easy matter. If counselling is concerned with the art of relationships, it is perhaps most challenged in working with the most deeply personal relationship any of us have, that with God through prayer. The God I encounter through another's description of their prayer may bear little relation to the one I meet in my own. I struggle, for example, over a God who listens only to prayers for others, but who is not interested in hearing the needs of the distressed and wounded person sitting in my room. There is the God who seems to enter into harsh judgements, such as in illness or bankruptcy, which he could withdraw if only the people concerned would live a more righteous life. There is the God who rejoices when a teenager destroys his treasured record collection because he has had a conversion experience, or the God who would like one of his people to die so that he can have another assistant in heaven. It is not that I do not recognise these images of God in my own psyche, but they do not accord with my experience at its most fundamental.

As counsellors, we must be aware that we too bring to the work our own incomplete images of God which may or may not be helpful, and it is perhaps at such times that we need to trust the skills which help us to empathise, to let be, and to facilitate another person to find out what they themselves really think and feel. It is in this way that a relationship will be formed which the other can then relate to their beliefs in a way which is meaningful for them. More often than not insight comes through relationship rather than the other way round. Thus, people will say, 'Because so-and-so acted lovingly towards me I suddenly realised that Jesus met people where they were', or 'It was through being loved that I began to hope that there might be a God who really was loving too.' The task of the counsellor is not to tell other people about God's love but to be with them in such a way that they can feel it and use it. This is prayer in action.

Nevertheless, prayer is often used explicitly as a means of offering the work to God for healing. This process cannot be rushed, and too often there is an assumption that prayer will 'fix' something which remains stuck because the emotions are stuck, leaving a person feeling perhaps worse than they did before. A young woman who had been raped told her counsellor that she was not willing to pray about it because she was not ready to let go of her hatred of men. It was part of her character formed by her experience and she needed it to survive. Some weeks later she found that she wanted to pray with the counsellor, and let the judgement go to God. This is perhaps a good example of the way in which we cannot bypass the emotional content of experience and apply religious doctrine neat to raw wounds, where it may only scar all the more deeply. Jesus did not preach to the sick and disturbed people who came to him, but healed them, and then let them draw their own conclusions about what this meant about him, and about their own relationship with God.

At the same time, there often comes a moment when something has been talked and felt through as far as it can be and something else is required in order for it to find its own level in a person's life. At such times, people may arrange for there to be some kind of service or may invent their own rituals. These frequently involve light or fire, food, or water, the archetypal constituents of ritual practice. A woman whose baby had died and who had no particular religious background visited the grave on the anniversary with candles and with Indian sweets which she had made. In this way, without having worked it out consciously, she was offering to the dead child symbols of life and nourishment, and at the same time honouring both her relationship as mother (in providing food) and her own connection with her ancestors, who were Indian.

There are points of contact between the practice of prayer and that of counselling at a deep level. Counsellors often describe their experience of working with people as maintaining an awareness of a sense of flow or something like a river running beneath the conversation taking place in the room. It is easy to lose touch with this when feeling anxious or under attack, or while trying too hard to do the right thing. Being able to become free of anxiety sufficiently to allow oneself to be sensitive to this dimension involves a curious mixture of exercising and letting go of one's own will, which is also very much part of the discipline of prayer. A nineteenth-century Russian priest and monk, Theophan the Recluse, writes about how important it is both to allow prayer to be spontaneous and to work at it. Eventually, if we do both these things, prayer will begin to flow of its own accord 'like a brook that murmurs in the heart'. One counsellor remembered being impressed as a child by his father's ability to pray spontaneously at family prayers. He himself, aged ten or eleven, would always lay out the books he wanted each day and read from them. From time to time, his father would suggest just saying a prayer off the top of his head but he could not. The most he could manage was 'God bless Mummy, God bless Daddy . . . ' and a list of other names. It was only as an adult, when he began to realise the crucial relevance of prayer in his own life, that he found he knew how to pray spontaneously. He rediscovered prayer as a gift, and also as the most fundamental ability he had as a human being.

This interplay between effort and spontaneity forms part of the experience of working with clients. A Jewish counsellor described how when she comes up against something which she finds hard to cope with in a session she tries to relax and contact a deeper level of wisdom. 'Hopefully,' she added, 'she answers.' Others finding themselves in such situations will use arrow prayers, short spontaneous requests for help, and may find a thought or idea will come into their mind as a result. Someone found herself asking for help in this way in a session with a client whose mood when they were together was always dark and angry. In that moment, her whole awareness shifted from the woman's resistance to her fragility, and together they were able to name the depression which was making their work so difficult.

Working closely with people in pastoral counselling means living with a burden of anxiety and risk. We not only carry the knowledge of other people's distress but also can sometimes be acutely aware that a person is contemplating suicide or behaving in ways that are deeply self-destructive. Prayer in these situations may be experienced as a resource which contains and nourishes the counsellor as well as enabling him or her to accept the limitations of his or her power to intervene. A colleague spent many anxious months with a client who left every session threatening that she would not be back because she would have killed herself. This was very hard to contain, and the counsellor said that although she understood it at a psychological level, it was only through prayer and through trust that the client had her own relationship with God that she was able to live with this situation, knowing that ultimately it was in God's hands. Similarly, an addiction counsellor described how he may often feel like praying and pleading that a person will manage to stay sober, but he constantly has to accept that this is between the other person and his God, and that God's plan for this person may not coincide with what he as counsellor longs for.

Dilemmas between prayer and pastoral counselling

It would not occur to some pastoral counsellors to question the place of prayer in what they do. Prayer is so fundamental an aspect of their lives that it would make no sense to try to exclude it. It is generally the case, however, that as people enter more deeply into training in psychological theory and skills, it not only leads them to question their own beliefs, but can generate considerable anxiety about whether they should use prayer in their work as counsellors at any level, either explicitly with the client or in their own personal prayer. Discussions about such matters often generate a strong emotional charge, suggesting that the conflicts which arise affect people at a very deep level.

Take, for example, a person of prayer who trains as a person-centred counsellor. That training will, quite rightly, be focused on the autonomy of the client. It is the client who knows what hurts, and it is the counsellor's job to maintain the three core conditions of empathy, congruence and unconditional positive regard in the service of the client's coming into being as his or her authentic self. It is often the case, as for the founding father Carl Rogers himself, that that self has been wounded in its core identity and in its relationship with God through a harsh, dogmatic religious regime. Such a person may experience themselves as intrinsically sinful or unlovable and incapable of approaching a God who, if he is in any sense personal at all, is either extremely remote or constantly disapproving.

Suppose such a person asks the counsellor to begin the session with prayer. The first difficulty for the counsellor may be the implication that, being a better person than the client, she has more direct access to God. What she says in prayer may reveal a concept of God or perception of God's will which is entirely different from that of the client, and it is the client's agenda, not her own, which should be at the centre of their work. Furthermore, to pray in such a way may give the impression that all is not well with the client simply because this fierce and distant God is withholding good things. It is also all too easy for the counsellor's hopes to slip into the prayer, and for the assumption to be made that it is God's job, not ours, to put things right. Already, the core values of person-centred counselling, self-actualisation and the autonomy of the client are placed under threat. One way of overcoming this may be to invite the client to pray, and some find this helpful. For the diffident client, however, this could represent an unbearable pressure to perform; others may use it as an opportunity to express thoughts and feelings which they are reluctant to put directly to the counsellor. Is the counsellor then to assume this is material she can use, or not?

An experienced pastoral counsellor declared emphatically that she never prays with clients during sessions. I was then somewhat perplexed when she began talking about something that had gone on during prayer with a client. In our subsequent discussion, she realised that although she always prayed with people at the beginnings and ends of sessions, she called those parts of the hour 'prayer', and the middle bit 'counselling'. Hence, she never prayed with people *during* the counselling session. She was intrigued to identify her own mental fast footwork, which is an excellent example of one way in which people deal with difficult questions; that is, to put things in separate compartments. Unfortunately, this counsellor's strategy, not being explicit even to herself, may have been completely opaque to her clients. Nevertheless, compartmentalisation may well be both abstinent and prudent. The counsellor who says – consciously – to himself, 'Although I am a person of prayer, I do not know what the psychological effects of such prayer will be on the person in front of me, so I will treat this quite separately from the work I have been trained for', may be doing the client great service in helping him to find his own path to God. As a patient in an AIDS hospice said to the chaplain: 'We are looking for God, too, but not in the places where the churches have hidden him.'

For many years, having grown up in a vicarage, I had as little as possible to do with churches. During this time my aunt, who was very devout, continued to pray for me and frequently reminded me that she was doing so. I found this irritating and often felt that instead of thinking I should be going to church, she should pay more attention to the family problems which had been influential in my rejection of the family religion. In recent years, since my re-entry into church and especially since her death, I have realised that this was unfair on my part. What I saw was the surface phenomenon of her hopes for me, but beneath that was a real concern and depth which, because I was not participating in that world, I could not perceive.

It is awareness of this gap in communication which is, I think, the great contribution of psychological theory and skills to pastoral counselling. The disciplines of counselling train us to stand back, to discover the other's frame of reference and to make a real effort to enter into it, and to listen carefully to what they really have to say. We learn to be abstinent in our self-disclosure in order to allow space for the other to express themselves, and to construct tight boundaries of time and space around the encounter. These are very potent skills which encourage trust and are thus open to abuse. In themselves they are morally neutral, being also the key to successful advertising, coercion and torture. Thus, in the counselling world there is a great emphasis on the importance of contract, supervision, respect for the individual, and self-awareness. It is not for the counsellor to direct or influence clients, but to enable them to find their own solutions. If, therefore, one has any respect for prayer as a reality, how can it be introduced without cutting across these basic precepts? In probing the unconscious of another we are already entering into their life in ways that are likely to be influential for good or ill. How then can we justify introducing another dimension, prayer, which opens up areas between us where we may find ourselves being deeply influential at an unconscious level, and which is also intensely personal? As one counsellor said when asked about this, 'Prayer is the antithesis of what I am trying to do.'

One solution to this dilemma is to treat the two worlds quite separately. Training usually results in a growth of consciousness which may lead a counsellor to question their own religious beliefs, and to find what was perhaps a natural trusting relationship with God thrown into confusion and turmoil. At such times, it may feel safer, if not imperative, to keep client work quite separate from one's prayer life. For some, opening gateways to the unconscious can be an experience of growth and deepening of faith, resulting in its becoming a more living reality in their lives; for others, insight into psychological processes may cast doubt on the possibility of believing anything. At such times, counsellors may feel that they need to treat their work as something they do involving a particular set of skills, and which has nothing to do with their religious life. This can be a helpful stage which enables a person to hone their skills as a counsellor before addressing the more complex problem of how this relates to faith. Sooner or later, however, it is likely that some crisis will occur which will force them to question the deep structure of their work: a failure perhaps, or a suicide, a client who is particularly difficult, or personal problems or stress. At such times counsellors need to question not only their techniques and professional expertise, but also what it is they believe in which keeps them in this kind of work and gives it meaning.

Prayer, of course, provides no guarantees. Like counselling itself, it involves setting out on a journey into the unknown, where we discover new knowledge and find ourselves accountable for what we do with it. A counsellor in a hospital chaplaincy found her beliefs profoundly changed by working with a dying man and his family, all of whom were convinced atheists. As an evangelical Christian she found this difficult although she had great respect for their integrity. Her prayer during this time was for help for herself as counsellor. On the night the man died she was with the family, and one of the daughters asked her if she thought her father would go to hell because he did not believe in God. She found herself replying with another question: 'You wouldn't send your father to hell, would you?', and following this with the statement that she did not believe God would either. This experience remained with her as one in which the interaction between prayer and the counselling relationship had changed her beliefs. For as an evangelical Christian she had always believed it was necessary to confess faith in Christ before death in order to be saved, but she found that she no longer believed this.

Prayer involves not only a growing self-awareness but also knowledge of other people. As we take others into our lives and pray for them, we are often given insight into their lives at a deep level, and we experience what Martin Israel has called 'tender soul contact' (Israel 1993). During the final illness and death of my mother, there were many people praying for her and for me, and this would surface into my life at unexpected moments as a sense of being cared for and nourished. There were also one or two people who did not know the immediate circumstances, but who were close to me in other ways and who spontaneously got in touch around that time to say that I had been very much on their minds and to ask what was going on. This level of communication is, of course, a two-way process in the intimacy of the counselling relationship. When I cancelled sessions with clients immediately after my mother's death some of those who wrote said they were relieved to know what the problem was, as they had sensed all was not well. Although my sudden absence raised various issues in the transference which needed working through on my return to work, the immediate responses to the death by the clients I had abandoned was an experience of true mutuality which was both humbling and heart-warming.

Even more complex, perhaps, in the context of counselling is the fact that although a regular discipline of prayer may nurture our sense of 'the brook that murmurs in the heart', it is also well documented that the life of prayer involves living with doubt, anxiety and the felt absence of God. Any travelling soul will experience its dark nights. Sometimes one approaches the familiar door and it appears tightly closed. For anyone who experiences prayer as a central and sustaining influence in their work this can be extremely frightening and disturbing. It requires us to think carefully about what we are prepared to say in a context where whatever is said is likely to be taken very seriously, and also challenges us to use the experience of doubt creatively. Jung's lifelong interest in the dark side of God arose from his exasperation with his pastor father's refusal to discuss the difficult questions of faith. Sometimes it is only the space and freedom created by doubt which makes it possible for us to believe.

Reservations as to the suitability of combining prayer with counselling usually arise from a respect for their respective potency. The wife of a rabbi, involved in pastoral counselling in her community, said it made her anxious to talk about praying for clients. Yet, she said, she would 'think about them prayerfully'. She went on to wonder how we would distinguish between praying for someone and thinking about them, and concluded that she would call it prayer when 'something had moved inside herself' in relation to the situation. This comment perhaps holds the key to the question of what it might mean to pray for another in the context of pastoral counselling.

There are, I believe, forms of intercession or praying for others which are a particular gift, and which are deeply influential in healing and changing the circumstances of people's lives. Through such prayers illnesses are cured, prisoners released, hearts are changed, and money becomes available for humanitarian projects. Counselling is not like this. Counsellor and client enter together into a situation in which the outcome cannot be prejudged. Each brings to it a certain experience and a certain expertise, and the mixture may be creative. It is not for us, as counsellors, to decide what is best for another or to pray or even hope for it. Ours is a stance of waiting and loving attention, trusting that if we can open ourselves and our relationships to God this will allow us to respond to the workings of grace. We have to be aware that at any stage our own perceptions may be disastrously wrong. The women who went with spices to the tomb of Jesus on Easter morning were reacting with utter appropriateness to the death of someone they loved, yet they had completely misunderstood the situation, as the angel revealed when he asked them, 'Why do ye seek the living among the dead?' (Luke 24: 5). We ourselves can never know what is being worked out in the salvation of our own souls let alone that of another, and it is in respecting this mystery that we need to muster all that we are taught about holding back and letting be.

The influence of prayer on the pastoral counsellor

What might it mean when a counsellor prays for his or her clients in their daily life, perhaps naming them, or carrying them in their hearts to shared worship or specifically praying for those in particular difficulties? Some signposts are found by questioning the early Christian monastics, who constitute one of the many groups of people who have made prayer their primary project.

Much of the material which survives from these centuries is concerned with how to live according to the Gospel within a monastic community, and the key to this is prayer. The whole project of early Christian monasticism was an attempt not to withdraw from society, but to find ways of forging true relationships through the practice of prayer and ascetic struggle, such that this might act like a yeast in society itself. Their aim could be said to have something in common with the practice of pastoral counselling, which is often criticised for its intimate nature, and for not giving sufficient weight to social action and change. This criticism fails to take account not only of the pervasive influence of the counselling culture (not, admittedly, always a positive one) but also of the deep connectedness of all life, which is a central concept in all the great religions. So, the monk fighting temptation in the desert is fighting evil for the whole cosmos. Similarly, those whose particular gifts enable them to help individuals in depth should not believe that their work has no wider influence. For the Christian (and this will have resonances in the understanding of other faiths), 'In so far as you have done this to the least of these my children, you have done it unto me' (Matthew 25: 40) can be taken to refer to the cosmic Christ through whom all things are created, and whose presence in all creation is the basis for our reverence for it.

'Prayer', wrote Theophan the Recluse, 'is the test of everything', and in the early Christian writings it is constantly emphasised that to try to achieve holiness by keeping away from close relationships is no answer. Indeed, Basil the Great, a fourth-century bishop and one of the founders of Eastern monasticism, said that someone trying to reach a state of perfection in isolation was like a carpenter trying to practise without touching wood (Spidlik 1992: 216). The early Fathers constantly remind us that prayer goes with good practice in relationships. When we have been hurt by another we are told we should make peace by speaking openly to him about it. Only if reconciliation is impossible should we take him into our prayer and, as Maximos the Confessor put it, 'pray for him sincerely without speaking ill of him to anyone' (in Palmer, Sherrard and Ware 1981: 104). In other words, it is in the difficulties of the encounters with other people, including our clients, that we come into contact with the wounds in our own souls. In allowing those wounds to be acknowledged and in offering them for healing we become able to enlarge the space between ourselves and the other in such a way that grace itself can act.

One day my supervisor asked how prayer entered into a situation where I was worried about a client on two counts. She was unwell and I suspected this might be serious. I was also having difficulty containing my irritation in our sessions. As far as the first problem was concerned there was nothing directly I could do, and it seemed to me a question of maintaining awareness, bearing this illness in mind at times of prayer, but not seeking any particular outcome. The second aspect, my own response or countertransference, was less straightforward and relates to the tradition of prayer cultivated by the early ascetics in the desert. The path they chose, involving fasting, living in uncomfortable and often hostile conditions, struggling to maintain godly relationships in community, was a way of cultivating trust in God rather than in oneself. Becoming aware of one's limitations and fragility as a created being, one learned to place one's reliance on the Creator. It was a way of becoming open to God, and suffused by his energies. Prayer in this sense has little to do with asking, and everything to do with allowing oneself to become a living manifestation of God's love. Thus, to allow oneself to become angry or envious or driven by desire gets in the way.

Similarly, acknowledging our own negative reactions and taking them into prayer can be a form of praying for others. In my own situation with this particular client, prayer was significant in two ways. It provided a space within which I was able to develop a greater awareness of what it was in me that was causing me to react as I was, rather as one might do in therapy. At the same time, prayer reflected back to me the inappropriateness of my reaction in the context of another person loved by God. The irritation did not disappear, but became something I could work with creatively in the relationship because I was no longer compelled by it. More often than not, prayer for another brings us back to ourselves, what we are contributing to a situation, and how we can change our response so that the other is set free.

Within the counselling session prayer in this sense may express itself in sitting with another's distress, neither intervening nor attempting to rescue. This can be one of the hardest things for trainee counsellors to learn. It places our own ego defences under great strain, because our natural instinct, if we can bear to come close at all, is to comfort and console. Yet, if we renounce that, we can find another way of being with the other which gives permission for deeper emotions and responses to emerge, and which can allow for a greater possibility of contact with that person's own depths. It may not be obvious at the time that this is happening, but if we can maintain our attention to the matter without defending against it the other will eventually be able to sense this and to be nourished by it. Often in such situations people will say things like, 'I couldn't respond at the time, but I knew you were there and that helped.' This kind of interaction is an echo of what the twentieth-century writer Simone Weil refers to when she says, 'Attention taken to its highest degree is the same thing as prayer. It presupposes faith and love' (Weil 1947/1952: 105).

At the end of my training I gave a lecture on these ideas, which had been the subject of my research project. Afterwards one of the tutors, not herself a Christian, said wryly, 'I did not know I had spent three years teaching you how to pray.' She had not. Counselling skills are not of themselves prayerful. What they can contribute is an improvement in our quality of attention to the other. Just as it is possible to meditate deeply without having any sense of a personal relationship with God, so it is possible to pay profound attention to another without having any faith which would lead one to call this prayerful. It is, however, difficult to understand how one can maintain such attention without being nourished by both love and some kind of faith against all the odds that this is worthwhile. This is what Weil points to when she says attention in the highest degree *presupposes* faith and love. At an ontological level – that is, at a level of what *is*, of being – such attention takes us into prayer because it takes us to and keeps us at a level of encounter which is deeper than we could ever hope to manage on our own. In this way, it could be said that the nature of the encounter in pastoral counselling is a prayerful one to the extent that it waits and hopes with full involvement.

Of itself, counselling psychology cannot take us to this level. It explains, it categorises, it gives us frameworks of understanding and various means of facilitating self-expression. The faith, theistic or atheistic, with which we underpin it operates independently of what we learn as professionals, and the integration of such faith with practice is a very individual matter. The conflicts which arise between the psychological and religious approaches will not go away. Indeed, they are likely to deepen as the secular counselling world becomes more and more interested in the spiritual dimension of human relationships. It is perhaps a key role of pastoral counsellors to face, at a very practical level, the profound and individual dilemmas involved in integrating psychological insight and prayer, whatever the traditions within which they practise.

REFERENCES

Ellenberger, H. (1970) *The Discovery of the Unconscious*, New York: Basic Books.

Israel, M. (1993) 'How do I pray?', *The Tablet*, 20 March: 362.

James, W. (1902/1982) *The Varieties of Religious Experience*, M.E. Marty (ed.), London: Penguin.

Oden, T. (1984) *Care of Souls in the Classical Tradition*, Philadelphia: Fortress.

Palmer, G., Sherrard, P. and Ware, K. (trans.) (1981) *The Philokalia*, vol. 2, London: Faber & Faber.

Spidlik, T. (1992) 'Basil the Great "The Greater Rules"', *Drinking from the Hidden Fountain: A Patristic Breviary*, London: New City.

Weil, S. (1947/1952) *Gravity and Grace* (trans. E. Crauford), London: Routledge and Kegan Paul.

5

ESTABLISHING THE THERAPEUTIC FRAME IN PASTORAL SETTINGS

Alan Boyd and Gordon Lynch

Introduction

A typical feature of the work of clergy and other pastoral carers within the Church is the relatively unstructured nature of their working environment. These pastoral workers meet people in a variety of different ways and in different settings, for example through a bereavement visit, or a baptismal visit, through an unsolicited knock at the minister's door or at the church door while saying farewells after the morning service. Any of these encounters may have started off with one intention but in the course of conversation previously hidden needs of the other person may become clear. Clergy and lay pastoral workers thus often find that they need to be flexible in their practice in order to respond appropriately to each specific pastoral situation.

This kind of flexibility clearly has its advantages, as it allows people to access care from the Church in a variety of ways. It is important to recognise, however, that there are significant tensions between the flexible and unstructured form that pastoral care normally takes in Britain and the more structured nature of the counselling relationship. Within counselling circles it is seen as an essential part of good practice that the counsellor and client have a working relationship characterised by clear boundaries and an explicit understanding of each of the parties' roles (e.g. British Association for Counselling 1998). This structure for the counselling relationship has been called the 'therapeutic frame' (Gray 1994). In the course of this chapter we will be looking to define and describe the therapeutic frame, identifying both the reasons why a clear therapeutic frame is important to counselling work and the key elements of a well-functioning therapeutic frame. Having established the nature and function of the therapeutic frame, we will then briefly consider how the concept of the therapeutic frame can help us to distinguish between pastoral counselling and pastoral care. We will also go on to discuss the potential difficulties of establishing an appropriate therapeutic frame within pastoral settings.

Defining the therapeutic frame

The therapeutic frame can be understood as the structures that establish the boundaries of the counselling relationship. In describing the therapeutic frame, Gray (1994) draws a useful analogy between it and a picture frame:

> When an artist completes a piece of work, it is usually framed and the choice of frame is important. If a decision is taken not to have a frame then the edge of the canvas will tell us where the imaginative work ends. When a frame is used, then it is this that performs the function of containing, the artistic creation has a boundary. Some artists have experimented with the idea of containment by letting parts of the picture spill over on to or beyond the frame, and it is only then that most of us become aware of its more usual function. . . . It is interesting that most artists prefer to have their work contained and when it is not the effect is disturbing, the eye concentrates more on what is not being contained than what is. Thus we might say that not to have a frame draws attention away from the main body of the creative work and simply functions to remind us that it is aesthetically more pleasing when it is contained.
>
> (1994: 5ff)

In the same way, then, that the picture frame preserves the viewer's focus on the picture, so the therapeutic frame enables the counsellor and their client to preserve an appropriate focus on their counselling work and to have a clear sense of where the counselling relationship begins and ends.

The therapeutic frame can be understood as consisting of two main elements. First, there are those parts of the therapeutic frame which are the subject of the explicit contract that a counsellor makes with their client. Within the counselling profession in Britain there is a widespread assumption that counsellors make explicit agreements with their clients about the terms on which the counsellor will offer the client counselling. Indeed, it is this explicit contract that makes the difference between a formal counselling relationship and other kinds of helping relationship in which counselling skills are used (see British Association for Counselling 1998). The specific issues that the counsellor and client will normally have to agree on in the counselling contract are the location of the counselling, the times when sessions will take place, the frequency and duration of the counselling sessions, what will happen in the event of the counsellor or client missing sessions (with or without prior notice), the fee that the client will be charged for receiving counselling and the degree of confidentiality which can be offered to the client.

The second main element of the therapeutic frame is issues that are not normally discussed when the counsellor and client establish their contract, but which are nevertheless essential for maintaining appropriate professional and therapeutic boundaries for the counselling relationship. These include the importance of the counselling room being a private and comfortable environment in which the counselling work can take place undisturbed. Also involved are certain boundaries that the counsellor imposes on their own behaviour with the client, such as refraining from engaging in a sexual relationship with their client or from giving advice. Guidance on the kind of boundaries that the counsellor should set on their behaviour with clients are generally given by the codes of ethics of relevant professional organisations (see, for example, British Psychological Society 1993; British Association for Counselling 1998). Another area is that of other actions on the counsellor's part which support their work with the client, such as the counsellor making good use of regular supervision of their work and the counsellor being able to make clear and realistic assessments of individuals' suitability for counselling with them. If a counselling relationship does not take place in a private and uninterrupted environment, or if the counsellor does not relate to their client in a consistent, ethical and professional way, then a significant threat will be posed to the framework of the counselling relationship and it is unlikely that the client will draw much benefit from it.

This understanding of the therapeutic frame is one that is adopted by most trained and accredited counsellors in Britain (see, for example, Bond 1993). As we will note later in the chapter, however, there can be significant obstacles to maintaining such a clear therapeutic frame for counselling in pastoral settings.

The therapeutic frame should not be understood as a set of rules which the counsellor imposes arbitrarily in order to impose their authority on the counselling relationship. Rather, it is possible to see the therapeutic frame as serving two essential functions within therapeutic relationships.

First, a clear therapeutic frame enables the counselling relationship to serve as a secure environment, or container, in which the client is enabled to explore their thoughts and experience feelings in increasing depth. Segal (1992) comments that the therapeutic frame is established when the counsellor shows themselves to be trustworthy and professionally disciplined. Thus, if a client is able to recognise that their counsellor will relate to them in a consistent way – for example, with regard to how long the counselling sessions are – and feels that their privacy is protected in the counselling relationship, then they are far more likely to be prepared to disclose deeper and more private information about themselves. If a counsellor does not set clear and consistent boundaries for their counselling relationships this can leave their clients feeling out of control and uncertain about the nature of the relationship that they have with the counsellor. This uncertainty is likely to make the client wary about sharing any significant personal information with the counsellor or about getting too closely in touch with painful or distressing emotions in the counselling room.

Case example: Diane

This point can be illustrated in the following case example.

> Diane was receiving counselling from the minister of a church other than the one that she normally attended. At first, Diane found her counselling very helpful. Her counsellor was warm and empathic, and she felt able to talk about parts of her life which she was currently finding difficult and upsetting. As the counselling relationship went on, however, Diane began to realise that the length of the sessions varied. Usually this happened if she became upset towards the end of a session, and her counsellor would then add another ten or fifteen minutes to the session so that she could feel better before they ended. At other times, though, her counsellor seemed to extend the session if he felt that they had not had enough time to explore a particular issue. At first, this made Diane feel pleased that her counsellor was so sensitive to her needs. But as time passed, she began to feel less in control in the sessions because she was not sure when they were going to end. The worst time was when she became upset towards the end of the session, and her counsellor told her that they would have to end on time that day as he had another appointment

that he had to go on to after they had finished. As the counselling relationship went on, Diane found that she was becoming more and more reluctant to share any really personal issues with her counsellor. She started to miss sessions, and eventually stopped going altogether. In this case, the inconsistency of the counsellor with regard to time boundaries ultimately undermined the work that he was doing with this client. Whilst it might have been difficult for the counsellor to end his sessions with Diane when she was still visibly distressed, in the longer term he would have provided a far more containing and therapeutic relationship for Diane if he had offered her consistent boundaries.

The therapeutic frame is supported in part by the formal contract the client and counsellor have entered into and it engages the adult part of both their psyches, which co-operates in a mature relationship to find healing. This allows the client to feel potentially negative and destructive feelings but have them contained within a safe relationship and it allows the counsellor to look at these feelings, discuss them and try to put them in context. Under other circumstances this would be quite a difficult thing to do within the Church, where anger, envy, sexual desire and self-loathing are often frowned upon, hidden and not talked about, and where the client may therefore be inhibited from showing their negative feelings.

Creating the therapeutic frame is important not only for building an environment in which the client can feel safe and secure, however. Psychodynamic counsellors, in particular, emphasise that a clear therapeutic framework between the counsellor and the client allows the feelings and patterns of earlier relationships in the client's life to re-emerge and to be played out in the counsellor–client relationship. The counsellor is therefore working with more than just the feelings, words and stories that the client brings. These are set against the backdrop of the therapeutic frame as a reference point by which to understand what the client is saying or doing. McLoughlin (1995), talking about the importance of boundaries, says that:

> The three areas of money, time and space all lend themselves as metaphors to divulge the client's communications about his experience of himself in relation to others. One or all of these areas may be used to refer to his inner world experience.
>
> (1995: 35)

Case example: Stan

The following case example illustrates this point.

> A counsellor, Sue, and her client, Stan, had been seeing each other on a weekly basis for a period of some months. One week, Stan forgot to bring his cheque to pay for the previous month's sessions and did not make any apology at the beginning of the session, believing that he could bring the cheque the following week. If, in this instance, Sue had not negotiated a clear system for the payment of the counselling fee, then any meaning behind Stan's action would have been missed. Because a clear agreement had been made between Sue and Stan about the date when fees should be paid, it was possible for them to think together about the significance of how he had dealt with his omission. It transpired that Stan hated to make explanations because that appeared in his eyes to be making snivelling excuses and he did not want to run, as he imagined it, the gauntlet of Sue's authoritarian reaction, which had its roots in the way his parents reacted. If the therapeutic frame had not been properly in place it would have been very difficult to have talked about or interpreted this incident, and an important source of learning would have been lost for both the counsellor and the client.

In summary, then, the therapeutic frame can be understood as the set of structures that establish and maintain appropriate boundaries for the counselling relationship. The therapeutic frame can be seen as including both elements which are the subject of the explicit contract between the counsellor and client, and elements which may not explicitly be spoken about between the counsellor and client but which reinforce the professional nature of the counselling relationship. The clinical value of the therapeutic frame can be seen, first, in its importance for maintaining the counselling relationship as a secure, consistent and contained environment in which clients are able to disclose very personal material and experience painful feelings. Second, from a psychodynamic perspective, the therapeutic frame can be used as a focus for learning about how the client relates to limits and structures in their life, which in turn might enable the counsellor and client to learn more about how the client's early experience influences their interactions with others in adult life.

Differentiating between pastoral care and pastoral counselling

A clear understanding of the therapeutic frame is one resource that can help pastoral practitioners to distinguish whether they are acting as pastoral counsellors or pastoral carers in their relationships with particular clients. In making this distinction it is important to recognise that 'pastoral care' is a difficult term to define, and that it can embrace a wide range of interactions from pastoral conversations between individuals to corporate forms of pastoral care expressed through liturgy, worship and social action (Pattison 1993). Furthermore, 'pastoral care' is arguably not simply the preserve of those formally recognised as ordained or lay pastoral workers by particular religious institutions. Rather, all members of religious communities can be understood to be involved in 'praxis' that is shaped and informed by the religious tradition that they adhere to (Graham 1996).

Whilst recognising the complexities in defining pastoral care, and identifying those who are involved in it, it is still possible to use the notion of the therapeutic frame to understand some of the differences between pastoral counselling and pastoral care that is undertaken by recognised pastoral workers with individual clients or parishioners. The content of the conversations that a pastoral counsellor and a pastoral carer may have with their clients may be very similar (e.g. focusing on the client's experience of bereavement), and there may also be a considerable degree of overlap in the skills that these practitioners use in their work. There is in reality, however, an important difference between these two kinds of helping relationship that derives from the way in which the boundaries of the relationship are structured. Pastoral counselling is a helping relationship based on an explicitly agreed, firm set of boundaries. Pastoral care, on the other hand, is a form of helping relationship in which the boundaries of the relationship are typically left unspoken and can often be more flexible than those of the pastoral counsellor. The differences in the way that these two types of pastoral relationship approach the issue of structure and boundaries can be summarised as shown in the table below.

Thus, whilst the content of the work and the practitioner skills involved in pastoral counselling and individual pastoral care may be very similar, there are some significant differences in the way that these relationships are set up and structured. These different formats each have their own inherent advantages and disadvantages. The clear framework of the pastoral counselling relationship can provide greater security and consistency to the client who wishes to explore their thoughts and

Pastoral counselling	Pastoral care
Involves an explicit contract or agreement between the counsellor and client on the terms on which they will work together.	Does not normally involve any explicit contract between the pastoral carer and their client.
The time, duration and frequency of the counselling sessions are agreed by the counsellor and client at the outset of the counselling relationship.	The time, duration and frequency of the meetings between the pastoral carer and their client are typically flexible.
A clear agreement is made between the counsellor and client concerning the degree of confidentiality that the counsellor is able to offer to the client.	There is not normally any explicit understanding between the pastoral carer and their client concerning the confidentiality of their relationship.
May involve the charging of a fee.	Does not usually involve a fee.
Counsellors require regular supervision from a person who is themself a trained and experienced counsellor.	Pastoral carers may or may not receive regular supervision of their work; this supervision would not necessarily be with someone who is a trained counsellor.

feelings at a deep level over a period of time. At the same time, the flexibility of the individual pastoral care relationship is advantageous in that it allows clients an easier access to immediate support, which may be very important in crisis situations. One disadvantage of the clear therapeutic frame in pastoral counselling is that some clients, who do not understand the purpose of the frame, may experience it as unnecessarily restrictive and punitive. Equally, a disadvantage of the flexibility of the individual pastoral care relationship is that it can be difficult for the pastoral carer to set any boundaries in their work, which can lead to a level of expectation and demand from clients which becomes an unbearable strain on the carer's own emotional resources. Pastoral relationships in general, though, will be better served if pastoral practitioners have a clear understanding of the capacity in which they are relating to a particular client (i.e. as a pastoral counsellor or a pastoral carer), and understand what boundaries are appropriate to the kind of relationship that they are engaged in.

Establishing the therapeutic frame in the pastoral setting

If we accept that a clear therapeutic frame is fundamental to effective and professional counselling practice, then it is important to explore what difficulties may arise for the pastoral counsellor when they attempt to establish such a clear frame for their own work. In order to think about these issues we will now look in turn at a few of the key elements of the therapeutic frame, and consider what problems may be associated with each of them for those who offer counselling in pastoral settings. The particular issues to be explored here will be the physical location of the counselling, the boundaries of confidentiality for the counselling relationship, the charging of a fee for the counselling work, and supervision. In exploring each of these areas very briefly, the aim here is to highlight how established pastoral practices and the wider culture of the Church can raise significant difficulties for establishing appropriate frameworks for pastoral counselling relationships.

The physical environment of the counselling relationship

The setting in which the pastoral counselling takes place is very important. It needs to be private and free from interruptions, and should be discreetly furnished and decorated so as not to be threatening to the client. It is of paramount importance that the counsellor and client are undisturbed in their work for the client to feel secure enough to start working at some depth. There are, consequently, a number of questions that the pastoral counsellor needs to bear in mind concerning the location of their counselling work. For example, what messages are implicitly communicated by the setting in which the counselling takes place? Is the setting of the counselling likely to be free from external interruptions? Who can see the client arriving at the session, and who greets them when they arrive at where the counselling is to take place?

Some venues in which pastoral counselling takes place have clear difficulties associated with them. For example, if a member of the clergy offers counselling to clients in the study of their vicarage or manse, they may be subject to being disturbed by the telephone or by other callers to their house. Furthermore, counselling a client in a book-lined room may convey the implicit message that the counsellor is scholarly and knowledgeable, and encourage deference on the client's part to the counsellor's 'expertise'. Similarly, if a pastoral counsellor works with someone in the sitting room of their house this can lead to possible confusion for the client, at an unconscious level, as to whether their relationship with the counsellor is a professional counselling relationship or something more informal and cosy. An ideal is for pastoral counselling to take place in rooms specially set aside for this purpose, which are private and free from outside interruptions. If a pastoral counsellor finds that they are unable to work in such an ideal setting, then it becomes important for them to reflect on what negative impact their environment may have on their counselling work and to consider how (if at all) these negative effects could be managed.

Confidentiality

Clear boundaries of confidentiality are essential in offering clients a framework in which they can begin to feel able to disclose parts of their experience which they find confusing, distressing or shameful. Although, within the Church, the confessional has represented a well-established form of confidential inter-personal encounter for many centuries, there can be many difficulties associated with maintaining confidentiality in pastoral counselling.

For example, it may be difficult to preserve confidentiality appropriately within pastoral care teams. Members of the team may talk about their plans for the week ahead and whom they are seeing. It is important in this context to have agreed protocol for discussing the pastoral counselling each member of the team has in hand, and for members of the team to be clear about what level of information it is appropriate to share with their colleagues about their clients. Where there is an established culture in a team of disclosing a great deal of information about clients in order for other members to pray for them, it will be much harder for any one counsellor to attempt to set up tighter boundaries of confidentiality around their work which will preserve the therapeutic frame more effectively.

Another source of difficulty with regard to confidentiality is that the clergy's partner can often erroneously be thought of as an unpaid member of the pastoral team – a confidant and informal supervisor. This can lead to unprofessional breaks of confidentiality and produce pressures for the spouse. A similar area of conflict might arise if the partner of the client is a regular member of the counsellor's congregation, and the counsellor has to interact and find ways to be in their company which respect confidentiality and the therapeutic frame. It is very difficult for one Church worker to fulfil the whole complex set of roles that are expected with the congregation, and this may raise the question as to the extent to which it is possible for a pastoral counsellor to offer a secure therapeutic frame to someone within their own congregation.

The fee for the counselling

Although not all clients do pay directly for counselling services that they receive, the fee does have an important place in counselling work. Not only is it the right recompense for professional labour but it also creates the environment in which a working alliance can be created and reflected upon. Furthermore, clients are often more likely to be motivated to use counselling in an active and focused way if they are paying for it, than if they are receiving it free of charge. When sessions have been paid for and time reserved then a clear boundary has been established between the counsellor and the client. This is helpful in the pastoral setting where boundaries are often unclear. It is also deeply symbolic about giving and withholding.

Charging a fee for pastoral counselling raises complex issues, however. If a pastoral counsellor charges a fee, then who retains it? If the pastoral counsellor is an ordained or lay worker within a congregation, does this mean that the church should receive the fee or should it be kept by the counsellor? If the client is a member of the pastoral counsellor's congregation, will this mean that the client assumes that they have a right to receive the counselling free of charge as part of the church's system of pastoral care? Or may the client, in this instance, feel that they have already paid for their counselling through their regular giving to the church? If the client does not pay a fee, then what financial support will the pastoral counsellor receive to enable them to pay for regular supervision of their work? Does charging a fee mean that some clients may not be able to afford counselling, or is it more useful to charge a fee to ensure that clients are well-motivated enough to engage in counselling?

The idea of charging a fee for pastoral services in the Church can seem very uncomfortable to pastoral practitioners. There can usually be a presumption within the Church that pastoral care and counselling, as well as other services, should be offered free of charge as part of the Church's mission to care. This assumption can make it very difficult for pastoral counsellors to make realistic decisions about whether or not it is appropriate for them to charge clients in their particular setting, and reflects a wider tension between setting clear boundaries in pastoral work and common assumptions in the Church about the form of a truly caring relationship. We shall return to this wider issue shortly.

Supervision

Regular supervision of a counsellor's practice by an experienced counsellor is now widely recognised as a fundamental aspect of a professional approach to counselling. When functioning properly, the supervisory relationship helps the counsellor to think about, and be supported in, their work with clients. The supervisory relationship can also function as an essential means of monitoring that the counsellor is maintaining an appropriate therapeutic frame with their clients.

Whilst some pastoral counsellors receive appropriate supervision of their work, others may not. For clergy generally, there is often little supervisory support of their pastoral work. If clergy engage in pastoral counselling as part of their ministry, they may well not receive any formal supervision of this counselling work unless they actively seek it out for themselves. Other pastoral counsellors may find themselves in a situation where their work is supervised by another pastoral practitioner who is not themself a trained counsellor. As Machin (1998) notes, when counsellors are supervised by colleagues who have little understanding of the nature and process of counselling, let alone of the nature and process of counselling supervision, this can leave the counsellor in the situation where their work is not being properly monitored or under-stood. In situations where pastoral counsellors are unsupervised in their work, or receive supervision that is inadequate in terms of its quantity or quality, then a central safeguard is lacking for ensuring that the counsellor is maintaining appropriate boundaries in their work with clients.

These four areas have been discussed here not because they are more problematic in terms of establishing and maintaining the therapeutic frame in pastoral settings than any other aspect of the frame. Rather, these four issues have been chosen as illustrative of wider tensions that emerge in attempting to set clear frameworks for pastoral counselling relationships in the context of religious organisations which have often emphasised the importance of informality and going the extra mile over setting clear boundaries. In considering, then, the difficulties that the pastoral counsellor may experience in attempting to establish a clear therapeutic frame for their work, it is important to recognise wider cultural and theological factors which influence this process.

For example, whilst it may be possible to define the therapeutic frame with reasonable clarity, the 'ministerial frame' is a far more diffuse and complex phenomenon. The liturgy for ordination within the Church of England states that the minister is 'called by God to be the servant and shepherd among the people to whom he or she is called'. The service goes on to describe the various tasks and roles the minister is expected to perform; among them is to call hearers to repentance, absolve sins and lead his or her people in prayer and worship. The note of ownership is interesting and must have an impact on the clergy self-image and sense of responsibility. This understanding of the work of the ordained minister leads many clergy to think that they have to be 'all things to all people'. This is a delicate if not impossible task. It seems that some clergy have taken 'all things to all people' as their principal way of relating, which has serious problems and deficiencies. Indeed, this way of being with others can bring clergy to the point where they lose their own personal boundaries at the expense of being somehow acceptable to the other.

Where clergy or lay pastoral workers lack a clear sense of their role, the danger arises that their sense of value in relation to their work derives mainly from how their parishioners or clients relate to them. This, in turn, can make it harder for the pastoral practitioner to impose limits or boundaries with those with whom they work, because some parishioners or clients are likely to find these boundaries frustrating. Such frustration, if managed appropriately and empathically by the pastoral practitioner, can actually be beneficial for many clients. Nevertheless, if a pastoral practitioner's sense of self-esteem is grounded in whether or not their parishioners or clients see them as a kind and helpful person, it can be harder for that practitioner to act in a way that they think may make people become angry or frustrated with them. Indeed, such a practitioner is more prone to see the imposition of (potentially frustrating) boundaries on the therapeutic relationship as a harsh or unloving act, rather than to recognise the usefulness of boundaries in containing therapeutic work. A lack of clarity in pastoral practitioners' understanding of their role in working with clients and parishioners, and a naïve view of love which neglects the importance of structure and boundaries in relationships, can therefore both militate against the establishment of a clear therapeutic frame in pastoral counselling work.

In reflecting on what resources can assist the pastoral counsellor to establish an appropriate therapeutic frame in their counselling work, a number of areas can be identified. First, it is crucial that the pastoral counsellor receives effective supervision from a supervisor who is themself a trained and experienced counsellor. Supervision can function as a means of thinking about how an appropriate therapeutic frame could be set up in the pastoral counsellor's particular context, and can also serve to monitor any actual or potential breaches of the frame. Second, it is important that the pastoral counsellor has a clear understanding of the nature and purpose of the professional boundaries of the counselling relationship. Books such as Gray (1994) and Bond (1993) can assist in this process, and most professional counselling training courses will devote some attention to these issues as well. Clarity over the rationale for applying boundaries in counselling may be particularly important for pastoral counsellors, who are naturally reluctant to impose them for fear of being unloving. Third, ongoing professional development can help pastoral counsellors to maintain an awareness of the importance of boundary issues in their work. Thus, contact with other pastoral counsellors, for example through organisations such as the Association for Pastoral Care and Counselling or the Clinical Theology Association, can enable pastoral practitioners both to be aware of standards of good practice in counselling and to get an idea of how others seek to maintain professional boundaries in their own pastoral setting. Similarly, involvement with wider professional bodies such as the British Association for Counselling or the British Psychological Society can sustain and nurture the professional practice of pastoral counsellors. Key elements, therefore, in assisting pastoral counsellors to establish and maintain an appropriate therapeutic frame for their work are contact with competent supervisors and professional networks, and a clear understanding on the counsellor's part of the professional and ethical basis of their work.

Summary

In this chapter, then, the notion of the therapeutic frame in counselling has been defined and the function of the frame has been explored. It has also been suggested that the explicit and firm boundaries involved in the therapeutic frame for counselling represent one of the main ways in which it is possible to distinguish between pastoral counselling and pastoral care, in which boundaries are typically more implicit and flexible. Difficulties in establishing an appropriate therapeutic frame for counselling in pastoral settings have also been identified, and it has been suggested that pastoral practitioners' attempts to be 'all things to all people' can hinder the process of setting clear boundaries in their therapeutic work. Finally, resources for assisting the pastoral counsellor to establish and maintain the therapeutic frame in their work have been noted briefly. Inevitably, within the confines of this short chapter, there have been many issues raised here that merit more detailed discussion. The central thrust of this chapter in seeking to emphasise the nature and function of the therapeutic frame is an important one, however. For without clarity on these issues, the work of pastoral counsellors is likely to be far less effective than it might otherwise prove to be.

REFERENCES

BAC (British Association for Counselling) (1998) *Code of Ethics for Counsellors*, Rugby: BAC.
Bond, T. (1993) *Standards and Ethics for Counselling in Action*, London: Sage.

BPS (British Psychological Society) (1993) *Code of Conduct, Ethical Principles and Guidelines*, Leicester; BPS.

Graham, E. (1996) *Transforming Practice*, London: Mowbray.

Gray, A. (1994) *An Introduction to the Therapeutic Frame*, London: Routledge.

Machin, L. (1998) 'Grief counselling in context: multiple roles and professional compromise', *British Journal of Guidance and Counselling*, 26(3): 387–98.

McLoughlin, B. (1995) *Developing Psychodynamic Counselling*, London: Sage.

Pattison, S. (1993) *A Critique of Pastoral Care* (2nd edn), London: SCM.

Segal, J. (1992) *Melanie Klein (Key Figures in Counselling and Psychotherapy Series)*, London: Sage.

6

DUAL RELATIONSHIPS IN PASTORAL COUNSELLING

Gordon Lynch

Introduction

In the previous chapter of this book the idea of the therapeutic frame has been introduced and discussed in relation to the work of the pastoral counsellor. From this discussion it is clear that appropriate pastoral counselling practice needs to be based on careful reflection about the terms and setting within which pastoral counselling is offered.

This chapter builds on this discussion of the therapeutic frame by examining in more detail the specific issue of dual relationships in pastoral counselling. By 'dual relationships', I mean situations in which the pastoral counsellor has another kind of relationship with their client – for example, either as their minister or as a fellow member of the same congregation. This is a broader use of the term than occurs in some of the literature on this issue, in which 'dual relationships' are defined specifically as situations in which the counsellor intentionally develops an exploitative sexual or non-sexual relationship with their client to meet their own physical, psychological or financial needs (see, for example, Craig 1991). My interest in this chapter is not, however, simply in dual relationships that are clearly exploitative, but in any situation in which the pastoral counsellor has some other kind of contact with their client outside of the counselling relationship. The central issue to be explored in this chapter is whether any kind of dual relationship between a pastoral counsellor and their client presents insurmountable problems for those seeking to practise pastoral counselling in an ethical and responsible way.

Initially in this chapter, I will explore why it is important to think about dual relationships in pastoral counselling. Having done this, I will discuss in more detail some of the difficulties that are associated with dual relationships between counsellor and clients, and then also note arguments against a blanket prohibition of dual relationships in counselling. Finally, I will argue that it is essential that pastoral counsellors develop a reflective approach to the issue of dual relationships, and suggest that such reflection will be aided by a clear understanding of the role of the pastoral counsellor and of the role conflicts that may be associated with dual relationships.

Why think about this issue?

To think that there may be anything problematic about dual relationships in counselling practice is a comparatively recent development. As Clarkson (1995) observes, most of the pioneering figures in counselling and psychotherapy had either sexual or non-sexual dual relationships with some of their clients. Freud's patients were drawn from a small social circle of middle-class Vienna, in which he knew either his patients or their families in other contexts. Ferenczi took holidays with some of his patients. Perls, Jung and Rogers are known to have had sexual relationships with current or former clients.

Over the past two decades, however, there has been a dramatic increase in the academic and popular recognition of the abuse that can be suffered by people who are the more vulnerable and powerless participants in a relationship. Initially, this took the form of an increased awareness of the reality of the psychological, physical and sexual abuse of children by adults. More recently, there has also been greater recognition of the abuse that can be experienced by people in the context of relationships with professionals such as doctors, social workers, lawyers, psychotherapists and ministers (see Rutter 1989; Fortune 1989). As more has become known about the professional abuse of clients it has become clear that dual relationships between professionals and their clients significantly increase the possibility of inappropriate or damaging behaviour on the part of the professional, whether such behaviour is intentionally exploitative or not. As Bader (1994) reports, dual relationships are a major cause of disciplinary actions against American psychotherapists and are also the source of the greatest losses for psychotherapists in malpractice lawsuits.

Quite why dual relationships are so problematic is something that will be explored later in this chapter. It is clear, however, that dual relationships are not at all uncommon among pastoral counsellors and their clients. Partly this is due to the fact that, with a comparatively small number of the population being involved in church congregations or other religious organisations, it is more likely that a pastoral counsellor will know their client in another context. This is made increasingly likely given that the network of those involved in churches or other religious groups is generally divided into discrete sub-groups in which people relate mostly to others who share a similar denominational background or theological outlook. Furthermore, whilst a large amount of pastoral counselling takes place in specialised centres or agencies, there is also a great deal of pastoral counselling work which is conducted within individual congregations either by the minister of that congregation or by nominated lay people within it. Such use of counselling as a means of pastoral support within individual congregations can draw theoretical support from 'holistic' models of pastoral care which advocate the provision of a range of different forms of caring practice within the congregation (see, for example, Lambourne 1983). Clearly, however, this use of counselling within individual congregations makes dual relationships between the counsellor and their client virtually inevitable.

Despite the frequency of dual relationships in pastoral counselling, there are often few resources to help pastoral counsellors to think seriously about the issues that such dual relationships present. This reflects a wider problem in the Church in terms of reflection about the appropriate boundaries of pastoral care. Those who work as ordained ministers have often not had any substantial training in professional ethics, and unlike many other professions they do not have access to clear ethical codes to guide their practice. Pastoral ministry is also typically compounded by a lack of clarity about the nature and limitations of role of the ordained minister, leaving ministers pulled about by the different demands of their job like 'a stray dog at a whistler's convention' (Craig 1991: 50). Indeed, even within the organisational structures of the Church, there can be an uncritical use of relationships involving significant role conflict, with ministers' pastoral support often offered by those who have some managerial responsibility over them (Kunst 1993). A further obstacle within the Church for critical reflection about the proper boundaries of pastoral care and counselling is a naïve theological emphasis on love, which can suggest that well-intentioned acts of caring do not need careful critical scrutiny and that the use of clear boundaries in caring work is in some sense harsh and unloving. Thus, within both the culture and the organisational structures of the Church, there can be a lack of reflection about issues relating to professional boundaries or role conflict that makes it harder for the pastoral counsellor to think effectively about the difficulties of dual relationships in their own work.

Given both the ethical difficulties inherent in dual relationships between counsellors and clients, and the frequency of dual relationships in counselling in pastoral settings, the issue of dual relationships in pastoral counselling needs to be the focus of a serious, ongoing discussion. Part of the contribution to this discussion to be made by this chapter is to highlight problems associated with dual relationships, and it is to this area that we will now turn.

The problems of dual relationships in pastoral counselling

If we are to think seriously about the ethical and therapeutic viability of dual relationships in pastoral counselling, it is important that the potential difficulties in such relationships are clearly understood. These difficulties can be understood in terms of breaches of the appropriate boundaries of the counselling relationship, with the distinction between what is appropriate inside and outside of a counselling relationship becoming blurred. For the purposes of this chapter, I want to focus on five particular areas of difficulty that are thrown up by dual relationships in pastoral counselling.

First, if a dual relationship exists between a pastoral counsellor and their client, there is a danger that the counsellor's or client's experience of that relationship may inappropriately influence their interaction in other settings. One important issue for the client is that they may develop a strong transference towards their counsellor which is not worked through in counselling, but has a powerful effect on the client's relationship with that counsellor outside of the counselling relationship. Consider the following case example:

A curate called Peter was experiencing severe personal and professional problems. He decided to seek counselling to help him reflect about these, and approached a senior clergyman in his diocese called Bob, whom he knew to be a warm and sensitive person. Bob agreed to offer Peter regular counselling, and they began to meet together. Peter was pleased at this arrangement as he had a great respect for Bob, and he found the experience of discussing his difficulties with him very helpful. After this counselling relationship had ended, Peter was also pleased that he continued to have contact with Bob in other settings and he still greatly valued Bob's insight and support. Some years later, Peter started seeing a psychotherapist as part of a professional psychotherapy training course that he was undertaking. In the course of this psychotherapy, Peter realised that he had very strong positive feelings towards Bob. He recognised that he loved and idealised him, and that in their contact over the many years since their counselling relationship had ended he had continually overvalued Bob's opinion of him and his work. Peter still sees Bob from time to time as part of his work within the Church, and he doubts that Bob has any real insight into the depth of feelings that he has towards him. Although his original counselling relationship with Bob seemed helpful, Peter realises now that it has left him with unresolved and unrealistic feelings which have been a source of great pain to him at times when he has perceived that Bob has rejected him or not been interested in him.

In this case example, the key problem is not that Peter developed a strong positive transference towards Bob which was not worked through in the counselling relationship. For in any successful short to medium-term counselling work, it is likely both that the client will develop some positive transference towards their counsellor and that it will not be possible or appropriate to discuss this fully in the counselling room (Lynch 1998). Rather, the central problem here is that because of the dual relationship between Peter and Bob this unresolved positive transference continued to exert a powerful and unspoken influence on Peter's feelings about himself and Bob for many years after their counselling relationship had ended. If Peter had had no contact with Bob outside of the counselling relationship, these idealised feelings would still have been present for him, but more probably these would have taken the form of a warm memory of the counselling relationship. As it was, however, Peter found for many years that his self-esteem remained powerfully affected by the way his former counsellor related to him in their subsequent meetings. If successful short- or medium-term pastoral counselling relationships do often evoke idealised feelings from the client towards the counsellor which cannot be worked through, then the question does arise as to whether it is appropriate for the counsellor to have contact with that client in another setting where those idealised feelings will continue to exert a powerful and unacknowledged influence on the client. In addition to this issue of unresolved idealised transference, problems can also arise if the client develops a negative transference towards their counsellor which they then act out in their relationship with that counsellor in another setting, or indeed if the counsellor develops a powerful countertransference towards the client which is acted out outside of counselling.

A second set of difficulties with dual relationships in pastoral counselling arise with the knowledge that the counsellor gains of their client in the confidential setting of counselling. It is widely accepted that counselling work should be conducted with the highest possible degree of confidentiality being given to the client's material (British Association for Counselling 1998). Dual relationships between a counsellor and client pose certain risks to these boundaries of confidentiality, however. For example, a counsellor who meets with their client in a context other than the counselling room may not be able to recall whether something that the client has told them was said in the confidential context of counselling or in another setting. This can lead to situations in which a counsellor inadvertently breaches confidentiality through not being clear whether information about the client is confidential or common knowledge. Ethical dilemmas can also arise for pastoral counsellors if they gain information about their clients through counselling which would then be highly pertinent to their involvement with the client outside of counselling (Craig 1991). For example, a counsellor working with someone from their own congregation might become aware that their client has previously used positions of authority inappropriately to meet their own emotional needs. If this client is then proposed for a leadership role within that congregation, the counsellor is then faced with an ethical dilemma. Should they speak up against this proposal because of the exploitative way that their client would be likely to make use of their leadership role, or should the counsellor's main responsibility be to preserve the confidentiality of the counselling relationship? For pastoral counsellors who are seeking to work within the British Association for Counselling *Code of Ethics for Counsellors* (1998), it is likely that a decision would usually be taken in favour of preserving confidentiality and thus not disclosing any information about the client. Such decisions are likely to be costly, however, both in terms of the stress that the counsellor faces in making such a decision and in terms of the stress that the counsellor will experience if they maintain their counselling relationship with that client.

A third difficulty with dual relationships in pastoral counselling concerns instances when behaviour appropriate to settings outside of counselling influences the counselling work inappropriately. The following case example illustrates such problems:

Kathy was a youth worker who was employed by a local church to run groups for young people in the congregation. Kathy and her husband had been experiencing problems in their relationship for some time, and this was known only to a few people in the congregation including the vicar, John. When things came to a head in Kathy's marriage, John, who was also a trained counsellor, rang Kathy to tell her that he wanted to offer her and her husband counselling about their difficulties. Kathy and her husband were happy to agree to this, as they both recognised that they would benefit from talking to another person about what decision they should take about their future. When John met with Kathy and her husband, he initiated what he described as a counselling session with them in which he told them that divorce was against what God wanted for them and that they should pray together to resolve their difficulties with each other. Kathy and her husband were feeling vulnerable and emotionally drained, and they had no energy to resist what John was saying or suggesting. After the session was over, however, they both felt angry and manipulated by the way John had dealt with them. Kathy and her husband subsequently decided to stay together, but also decided that they wanted to move to another local church because they were unhappy at the way John had dealt with them. Because John was an important and respected figure in the churches in that area, Kathy chose not to tell him the real reason for her leaving his church. Because of her work, she still sees him from time to time, and John still seems to think that his intervention was instrumental in keeping Kathy and her husband together.

At the heart of this case example is the fact that John's practice as a counsellor was inappropriately influenced by his normal style of pastoral interaction as a clergyman. It may be appropriate for a priest or minister to initiate pastoral contacts, and to offer direct moral or theological opinions as part of those contacts, but these are not appropriate behaviours for someone who is acting as a counsellor. Implicit in this case example would also seem to be a lack of clarity on John's part about the nature of an appropriate framework for counselling relationships. When a counsellor has a relationship with their client outside of the counselling room, it can become harder for them to distinguish what kinds of behaviour are appropriate to which relationship. This is certainly evident in this case example, with John unthinkingly conducting the counselling session as he would another kind of pastoral encounter. What is also striking from this example is that John never became aware of how his intervention had actually been experienced by Kathy and her husband.

This illustrates another difficulty with dual relationships in counselling, namely that clients may be far more reluctant to tell their counsellor about negative aspects of the counselling relationship if they have to work or socialise with them in another context.

A fourth difficulty with dual relationships in pastoral counselling concerns the client's knowledge of the counsellor gained from outside of the counselling relationship. If, for example, a pastoral counsellor works with other people from their same congregation, it is likely that their clients will have a reasonable knowledge of the counsellor's private life. Potentially, this could prove intrusive if the counselling process becomes focused on the client's knowledge of difficulties that the counsellor may be having, rather than on the client's own concerns. It may well be possible to work therapeutically with any associations or feelings that the client has in relation to counsellor difficulties, but it is easier for the counsellor to think clearly about the meaning of the client's material if such a confusion between the counsellor's and client's worlds does not exist.

A fifth source of difficulty with dual relationships concerns the potential for pastoral counsellors to seek, intentionally or unwittingly, to use clients to meet their own emotional needs. Kunst (1993) has argued that it is a common experience for priests and ordained clergy working in congregational settings to feel that they are giving out emotionally to others in the congregation but that these relationships are 'half-intimacies' in which their own emotional needs are unaddressed. This dissatisfaction can lead to creative action, in which clergy establish suitable support systems for themselves outside of the congregation, or more negatively it can lead to burn-out or an exploitative use of relationships with congregational members to meet emotional needs. For some pastoral counsellors whose emotional needs are unmet elsewhere, it can be tempting to encourage the intimacy of the counselling relationship in such ways that a friendship is developed between the counsellor and their client outside of the counselling sessions. When this occurs, clients may initially feel very pleased that their counsellor wants to have a friendship with them, but over time the fundamentally exploitative nature of the relationship is likely to become clearer, to the detriment of both parties (see, for example, Kagle and Giebelhausen 1994).

In this part of the chapter, I have highlighted only some of the risks that can be associated with dual relationships in pastoral counselling. It is worth recognising that all of these are present simultaneously whenever a pastoral counsellor engages in a dual relationship with a client. Consequently, whenever such a dual relationship occurs, the counsellor has many more things to reflect upon and monitor in addition to the existing complexities of working with clients. It should also be acknowledged that clients also often have an awareness of the problems of dual relationships and that this can lead them either to censor carefully the way they present themselves to a counsellor whom they know in another context or to opt only to seek help from professionals with whom they do not have a dual relationship (Hendriks 1991). From this catalogue of difficulties associated with dual relationships, it is clear that these can potentially involve at best a dilution of the effectiveness of the counselling process and at worst the unethical exploitation of the client to meet the counsellor's needs or the abuse of the client through inappropriate practice. This observation should lead us to question seriously whether dual relationships between pastoral counsellors and their clients are an appropriate form of practice.

Difficulties in prohibiting dual relationships

The difficulties associated with dual relationships in counselling lead some writers to advocate an absolute ban on any kind of dual relationship between counsellors and clients (Kagle and Giebelhausen 1994). Others, however, have suggested that such an absolutist stance is unhelpful and that it may be possible to work constructively with dual relationships if one has a clear understanding of their dangers (Clarkson 1995). One argument used to support this latter view is that dual relationships are extremely hard to avoid in certain settings. For example, in small rural communities it would be very difficult for clients not to know their counsellor in another context. Equally, in a small professional network such as the world of psychotherapy it can be very difficult for psychotherapists to avoid contact with their current or former therapists in other roles. As was noted earlier, religious networks are similarly often small, and it is not always easy to ensure that a pastoral counsellor does not know or would not meet their client in another context. To place an absolute ban on dual relationships would therefore make it very difficult both for counsellors to practise counselling, and for clients to have access to counselling, in the context of small social networks. For some clients, their only choice may be between receiving counselling where they know their counsellor in another context or not receiving counselling at all. It could, therefore, be argued that for a client in distress it is a lesser evil for them to have a dual relationship with someone who offers them counselling support, than for them not to be able to have any such support.

A second argument used against an absolute prohibition of dual relationships in counselling is that an inflexible adherence to such rules is likely to be more damaging than beneficial to clients. Hermansson (1997) argues that excessive rigidity or emotional distance on the part of the counsellor is a more common source of harm to clients than excessive closeness. He comments:

> Undoubtedly there is in some quarters an excessive zeal about boundary control which can lead to stances that seem overly precious and at times even arrogant in relation to clients and colleagues in the profession. The damage that has been done and can potentially be done through boundary violation gives some justification to this line of thinking and to the realistic need for caution. However, just tightening boundaries is also over-simplistic and has the added danger of possibly setting off from involvement the very qualities that make counselling therapeutic. What is left can be a pseudo-professional stance that is controlling in its effects and barren in its essence.
>
> (1997: 140)

If the essence of what is therapeutic about counselling is a human encounter in which the counsellor offers acceptance and engages empathically with the client, then an overscrupulous preoccupation with boundaries could arguably be seen as detracting from these human qualities.

A third, and more positive argument in favour of a more flexible and constructive approach to dual relationships in counselling is that such relationships have the potential to be actively therapeutic for clients. This is illustrated in the following case example:

> Jane was a young woman who had grown up in a children's home and who had a history of receiving psychiatric help for recurrent periods of depression. She started to attend a local church, and after a few months started seeing a pastoral counsellor based at that church. In addition to Jane's individual counselling sessions, she also met with her counsellor and a small group of other people to talk about their personal lives and to pray together. Jane greatly valued the support she received in her individual counselling, and also enjoyed meeting in the small group, which felt like some kind of informal family for her. Through the support of the counselling and the small group, Jane was able for a few years to be an active member of the local church. Although she continued to have difficulty with her

depression and eventually left the church, this period of time gave Jane an experience of belonging to a community of people that she had never had before and it remained one of the happier times of her life.

It could be argued that one of the potential benefits of pastoral counselling is precisely that it is practised as part of a wider social network of people who worship, pray, work and socialise together. If the pastoral counselling relationship can become integrated with other forms of support and social interaction within congregations or religious groups, then clients may be able to enjoy much richer opportunities for growth and development than if their experience of counselling is of an isolated helping relationship. A dual relationship with a pastoral counsellor may, then, for some clients, have the potential to deepen the therapeutic benefits both of the counselling and of other interactions that the client has within their congregation or religious community.

From these arguments it is clear that a simplistic and wholesale rejection of dual relationships in pastoral counselling could itself be in danger of putting the counsellor's need for a pure counselling frame-work ahead of the practical and psychological needs of their clients. At the same time, however, the problems with dual relationships that have been identified earlier in the chapter also represent significant threats to clients' interests and emotional well-being. What is needed, then, is a reflective approach to the issue of dual relationships in pastoral counselling which is able to balance their risks and possible benefits, and make an appropriate assessment of how clients may be most appropriately related to. In the final part of this chapter, some discussion will be given of resources that can help such a reflective approach.

Maintaining a reflective approach

An important first step in developing a critical and reflective approach to dual relationships in pastoral counselling, and indeed to boundary issues more generally, is to recognise how vital such reflection is. In any pastoral counselling relationship, it is always the counsellor's responsibility to act ethically in order to protect the client's interests and well-being. It is not sufficient for the counsellor to think that they have discharged this duty simply by acting out of good intentions for their client. In the case examples given earlier, both Bob and John presumably believed that they were acting in their client's best interests by offering counselling in the way that they did. Similarly, it is not adequate for counsellors to believe that they have acted appropriately simply because their clients do not explicitly tell them that they have not. Again, in the case examples involving Bob and John, their clients for different reasons did not feel able to say how harmful their experience of counselling had been for them. It is essential, then, for pastoral counsellors to be able to reflect critically on how the terms on which they provide counselling may affect their clients, rather than assume that good intentions on their part, or even positive reports from their clients, are sure signs of ethical and appropriate practice.

Critical reflection about dual relationships in pastoral counselling will be helped if pastoral practitioners have a clear understanding of their role and of the nature of the relationship that they are offering to their clients. In particular, it is important for pastoral practitioners to be clear about whether the help that they offer to others is actually counselling or whether it represents the use of counselling skills in the context of another role. Counselling has been defined by the British Association for Counselling as a relationship in which there is an explicit agreement between two people that they will function in that relationship as counsellor and client. As discussed in the previous chapter, this relationship is also typically characterised by clear and fixed agreements about the frequency, duration and location of the counselling sessions, and by an agreement about the degree of confidentiality in the relationship. By contrast, pastoral carers may use many of the skills that counsellors use, whilst not having these same explicit agreements with those with whom they work. The expectations, obligations and rights of such pastoral relationships will be therefore be defined largely by the role of the carer, whether that be a priest or minister or some form of lay pastoral worker, rather than by an explicit counselling contract. In certain key respects, the expectations, obligations and rights associated with the work of counsellors and with that of ordained or lay pastoral carers are different, and clarity about appropriate practice in a pastoral relationship will therefore rest upon clarity about the role that the pastoral practitioner is working in.

If pastoral practitioners have a clear understanding of what role they are occupying as they offer support to others, and within this clearly understand whether they are functioning as a counsellor or not, it will be easier to think about any role confusion or conflict that may arise in their work with clients. Kitchener (1988) has proposed that dual relationships become more problematic when there is a greater degree of role conflict involved across the two different relationships. She suggests that dual relationships are therefore more likely to be damaging:

1   when there is a greater degree of incompatibility of the *expectations* of the different roles;
2   when there is a greater degree of incompatibility of the *obligations and rights* of the different roles;
3   when there is greater *power and prestige* associated with the professional helper's role.

These points provide a helpful framework for thinking about the way in which a dual relationship between a pastoral counsellor and their client could present difficulties. For example, tensions can arise if there are very different expectations associated with the different relationships. Thus, if a client knows their counsellor as a fellow member of a prayer group, the client may expect their counsellor to talk about their own experience in the counselling session in the same way that the counsellor does as a member of the prayer group. Likewise, if a client is being counselled by their minister, they may expect that they can have the same degree of flexibility in their access to the minister's time as they would if they were seeking more informal pastoral support from the minister. With regard to the issue of obligations and rights, if a priest is receiving counselling from a senior clergy person who also has managerial responsibility for them, then a role conflict can arise between the counsellor's obligation to provide an accepting and confidential service and the manager's obligation to monitor, and if necessary intervene, in the practice of those whom they manage. Kitchener's framework also highlights that problems in dual relationships are likely to be exacebated where the counsellor's position is powerful or prestigious. In a pastoral context, then, when the client is counselled by someone who has power or prestige in their social network, such as a lay or ordained leader of their congregation, it becomes harder for the client to be able to resist or speak out about inappropriate practice that arises in the context of this dual relationship, and the effects of inappropriate practice are often more damaging.

   Thinking critically about dual relationships in pastoral counselling will therefore be helped if pastoral practitioners have both a clear understanding of the nature of their pastoral role and also a clear awareness of any role conflict that may ensue if they engage in a counselling relationship with someone whom they know in another context. This kind of awareness is very useful in helping pastoral carers and counsellors to think about the likely dangers of dual relationships with their clients, but of itself it is not enough to determine whether a particular dual relationship should be engaged in or not. Ultimately, each practitioner must make their own decision on whether dual relationships in pastoral counselling are ethically acceptable or not, and what kinds of dual relationship may be more preferable than others. An essential resource in facilitating such decision making is appropriate and skilful supervision, in which the supervisor helps the counsellor to reflect both about the professional issues involved in the maintenance of boundaries and about any transferential or countertransferential material that may be unconsciously influencing the counsellor's thinking on these issues.

Whilst wishing to encourage pastoral counsellors to be reflective in their approach to dual relationships with their clients, I still have a basic presumption against the usefulness of such relationships in pastoral counselling. To work effectively with clients is complex and potentially very demanding work, and to have a dual relationship with one's client is to add significantly to the already complex dynamics of the counselling relationship. It is difficult to imagine that a pastoral counsellor with minimal training or experience would be able satisfactorily to negotiate these complex dynamics in a way that was therapeutic for the client. Given how little is known generally about clients' experiences of receiving pastoral counselling, there is no substantial evidence that more experienced and well-trained pastoral counsellors can work with dual relationships in a way that is wholly beneficial for their clients either. Regardless of one's view, however, an ongoing debate is clearly needed on this issue to ensure that pastoral counsellors continue to develop a reflective approach to dual relationships rather than fall into the traps of unthinking and excessive legalism or of an unthinking and lax approach to therapeutic boundaries.

REFERENCES

BAC (British Association for Counselling) (1998) *Code of Ethics for Counsellors*, Rugby: BAC.

Bader, E. (1994) 'Dual relationships: legal and ethical trends', *Transactional Analysis Journal*, 24(1): 64–6.

Clarkson, P. (1995) *The Therapeutic Relationship*, London: Whurr.

Craig, J. (1991) 'Preventing dual relationships in pastoral counseling', *Counseling and Values*, 36(1): 49–54.

Fortune, M. (1989) *Is Nothing Sacred? When Sex Invades the Pastoral Relationship*, San Francisco: Harper & Row.

Hendriks, J. (1991) 'Looking for pastoral care anonymously', *Journal of Empirical Theology*, 4(1): 81–104.

Hermansson, G. (1997) 'Boundaries and boundary management in counselling: the never-ending story', *British Journal of Guidance and Counselling*, 25(2): 133–46.

Kagle, J. and Giebelhausen, P. (1994) 'Dual relationships and professional boundaries', *Social Work*, 39(2): 213–20.

Kitchener, K. (1988) 'Dual role relationships: what makes them so problematic?', *Journal of Counseling and Development*, 67: 217–21.

Kunst, J. (1993) 'A system malfunction: role conflict and the minister', *Journal of Psychology and Christianity*, 12(3): 205–13.

Lambourne, R. (1983) *Explorations in Health and Salvation*, Birmingham: University of Birmingham Press.

Lynch, G. (1998) 'The appication of self psychology to short-term counselling', *Psychodynamic Counselling*, 4(4): 473–85.

Rutter, P. (1989) *Sex in the Forbidden Zone*, London: Mandala.

7

TRANSFERENCE AND COUNTERTRANSFERENCE IN PASTORAL COUNSELLING

Barrie Hinksman

Introduction

In this chapter I shall explore some aspects of transference as they occur in the context of pastoral counselling and, in particular, examine some implications for a person seeking counselling when they work with a counsellor who is explicitly associated with a religious tradition or a religious organisation. First, I will set out some current understandings about transference and countertransference. The literature in this area is very large indeed. As will be seen later, there are those in the psychoanalytic tradition who consider that almost the whole work of analysis consists of analysing the phenomenon of transference. Without going to what they would consider such an extreme position, there are other psychotherapists and counsellors who would agree that much of their work can be done by focusing on the various aspects of the relationship between the psychotherapist and her client or patient, or between the counsellee and counsellor.

For the purposes of this chapter I shall use the word 'counselling' (in reference to pastoral counselling) to refer to work which, in my view, may extend into the realm of psychotherapy. In exploring the nature of transference and countertransference, I have chosen as a resource Petruska Clarkson's (1995) *The Therapeutic Relationship*. Her overview of the subject does justice to conflicting and variant views and so can be taken to represent the mainstream in counselling and psychotherapeutic practice. Clarkson's analysis of the therapeutic relationship into five related but quite distinguishable relationships (not all of which will necessarily be evident in every pastoral encounter) puts the transferential relationship into its context and goes beyond what this chapter can encompass.

Having established something about transference and counter-transference in the counselling setting, I turn to the matter of how a religious provenance might influence these phenomena. In doing so, I have attempted to look at the process from both ends (i.e. from the perspectives of the counsellor and of the counsellee). As well as seeking to explain the issues involved, I have given at a number of points some illustrations from practice. Whilst these are taken from experience (my own and that of colleagues with whom I have engaged in supervision), the details are, of course, altered so as to make them anonymous.

Defining transference and countertransference

The phenomena of transference are all around us. The core meaning of the experience of transference lies in the activity of transferring, in this instance, elements of one situation or relationship to another situation or relationship. In the same way, educationalists speak of a 'transfer of learning' from the classroom to life outside the school or college. In that process, the students take what they have learned within particular confines and, by trial and error, match their learning against new and often unforeseen situations. In the situation of pastoral (or any other kind of) counselling, what was learned once by the counsellee is carried into and matched or applied in another context. As we shall see, it may be that it would be more appropriate to speak of mismatching and misapplying, but the same general principle of (usually unwitting) trial and error is taking place. The major difference is that the transfer of learning is in part a conscious and deliberate exercise, although it is also the case that much of it 'just happens' (i.e. is not volitional or conscious). In the case of transference in a counselling setting, the transfer is most commonly of something not knowingly learned and the processes of matching and testing are also usually quite involuntary and out of awareness.

In the context of a pastoral counselling relationship, therefore, the term 'learning' has to be understood in at least two senses. Much of what happens is at the level of aware and explicit mental functioning: it is a process of learning, unlearning and learning anew in order to function in ways which are more useful, or more satisfying. This is how the counsellee comes to understand how her actions, responses, attitudes, emotional expressions, desires and those of other people are contributing to a situation which, we may assume, is troubling her.

A second sense of learning is to be found in areas of the counsellee's personhood which are usually thought of as lying deeper. 'Deeper' here does not necessarily indicate profundity (as in deep thought), but rather points to a kind of learning less open to immediate introspection. Such learning is best thought of as being out of awareness, or subconscious or unconscious. (These three terms are not meant to be equivalent. They represent quite different theories held by various schools of counselling or psychotherapeutic psychology. For present purposes, however, the differences are largely immaterial since all three suggest important personal material which is beyond the introspection of the counsellee, but which may become available to her through the counselling process.) The learning in this context is concerned most often with what have been termed 'infantile prototypes' (Laplanche and Pontalis 1988, cited in Clarkson 1995: 9–10). Classic examples of these infantile prototypes include mother and father figures. In the context of the counselling relationship the existence and influence of these prototypes become evident to the counsellor through the ways in which the counsellee approaches her. Very commonly they are evident in tones of voice and attitudes. Sometimes, there are discrete pieces of behaviour which are disclosive of transference, as when a person consistently tries to bend the boundaries of a meeting by arriving late or on the wrong day and then letting the counsellor know that they regard anything less than enthusiastic acceptance as injustice or wilful misunderstanding. Yet other counsellees may seek to ingratiate themselves as though the counsellor were some potentate whose whims must be anticipated, lest some undefined ills occur. What I am describing here is more than a one-off instance of something which may be purely random. I am pointing to patterns which may emerge but be evident only to the counsellor. From the point of view of the counsellee, the counsellor seems to be this or that kind of person and seems to expect or want certain kinds of behaviour or attitude. Many of us know the experience of thinking, 'I couldn't help noticing how she seemed irritated or tired on the occasion when I spoke of my feelings of depression: perhaps it would be best to keep these to myself, as I have learned from early childhood to do (mother's too busy now: you go and play with your friends).' On the other hand, 'when I talked about feelings of sadness when father was made redundant and took to drinking, my counsellor perked up visibly: perhaps this is the kind of thing I should concentrate on. It seems important to keep her interest.' These thoughts about the counsellor as a person may have little or nothing to do with the counsellor as she knows herself or as her friends might recognise her. It is salutary to remember, though, that there are frequently important overlaps which, were the information available, might enable even close friends to see their counsellor friend in a different light.

Laplanche and Pontalis's infantile prototypes referred to above have familiar names, names related to the family. The obvious familiar prototypes are mother and father. In discussing transference, they are usefully divided into good mother/bad mother and good father/bad father. This division is thought by many to be more than a verbal split but rather a split within the person who has that primitive experience. Her world is sundered by these conflicting experiences. Any counsellor who has experienced a catastrophic switch from positive to negative transference would find it easy to believe that they are experiencing some of the internal violence which the counsellee once experienced consciously and, existentially, always experiences in every situation, because it is one of the paradigms for organising her life. The good mother and good father experiences are referred to as positive transferences and their opposites as negative (Freud 1917/1991: 495). The terms 'positive' and 'negative' in this context do not indicate anything positive or negative about how the pastoral counselling is proceeding, nor should they be taken as proof of the actual parents' attitudes or activities. So, a positive maternal transference by a counsellee means that she is transferring on to the pastoral counsellor (male or female) warm, positive feelings *as if* the counsellor were engaging as a warm, accepting mother. These feelings arise from the learned experience of the counsellee. This is not to say that all warm and positive feelings towards the counsellor should be regarded as transferential. To grant that would be to behave in a reductionist manner whose effect is to render null any possibility that gratitude or warm regard have any intrinsic value specific to that moment or that relationship. Such a view runs counter to the theory and values of counselling. They are not proof that she ever had this experience, nor that she did not have it. They are a part of how she once wanted things to be with another person, quite possibly her mother. They are also reproduced in the counselling relationship, and perhaps frequently in some of her other relationships, indicating how she wants things to be with another person in order to reduce a felt deficit which is in her present.

This understanding of transference owes much to the study of the subject by psychoanalysts. Attempts to define transference and to work with it for the benefit of troubled people go back to Sigmund Freud. Freud noted how in analytic sessions people behaved towards him and towards his colleagues *as though* the analysts were someone other (Freud 1917/1991: 490ff). At an early stage in his thinking, he suggested that, for reasons including this one, it would be best for the analyst so to occlude his own personhood as to become only a mirror to the analysand. In that mirror the dramas of the infantile prototypes could be seen and analysed. And, even though Freud was sceptical about attempts to cure people in analysis, he, as a classical scholar, knew well the meanings of the Greek words he had employed for his new discipline of psychoanalysis – the unloosing of the soul. So much was transference (often referred to as 'the transference') a part of psychoanalytic work that some analysts came to regard its invocation, interpretation and resolution as synonymous with psychoanalysis. Freud did not say that there could be no analysis without transference because he recognised that there are people who, in the ordinary course of their lives, have worked through whatever needed to be worked through to the point where they did not obtrude their projections into other situations. Jung also held this view:

> The great importance of the transference has often led to the mistaken idea that it is absolutely indispensable for a cure, that it must be demanded from the patient, so to speak. But a thing like that can no more be demanded than faith, which is only valuable when it is spontaneous. Enforced faith is nothing but spiritual cramp. Anyone who thinks that he must 'demand' a transference is forgetting that this is only one of the therapeutic factors.
>
> (Jung, cited in Clarkson 1995: 11)

As the exploration and discussion of transference continued, it became apparent that the rather limited list of infantile prototypes did not do justice to the complexity of the experience. Other schools of counselling take different views of these matters (Clarkson 1995: 70–3). For example, if a counsellee feels towards the counsellor as though he were the ideal father (which he did not have in his upbringing), it may be simplistic or plain inaccurate to say this is no more than the projection or putting out of the counsellee's desire to have such an ideal father. Rather, it may be that the counsellee had a satisfactory father (not perfect, but good enough), and that what he is putting on to the counsellor is an idealised sense of *himself.* In other words, he sees in the counsellor the self he would like to be. In such instances, there may well be – and often is – some real similarity between aspects of the counsellor as a person and the person the counsellee would like to be. But to focus on the actual similarity would almost certainly be less helpful than to concentrate on what it is which the counsellee identifies and to work towards some owning of that projection ('that's how you're seeing me: is that how *you* would like to be?'). This is an example of a 'self–object transference'. The exploration of a range of these types of transference arises from the self-psychology school associated with writers such as Kohut and Wolf (Wolf 1988: 186–7, cited in Clarkson 1995: 69–70). Several such possibilities can be suggested, some of which may be understood as positive and others of which may be understood as variations of negative (albeit self–object) transference. Like the infantile prototype transferences, they are very often out of the counsellee's awareness, although they may come quite easily into awareness through the prompting of the counsellor.

The psychoanalytic relationship and the pastoral counselling relationship involve at least two people, the analyst and the analysand, and the counsellor and counsellee. (It is also the case that much important counselling and psychotherapeutic work is done in groups, either selected or referred client groups, work groups, couples or families.) If the counsellee is transferring infantile relationships or self–object transferences on to the counsellor and if this is a usual human activity, then we might expect some corresponding activity on the part of the counsellor. This latter is referred to as (the) countertransference. In considering countertransference, it is important to distinguish between what Clarkson (1995: 89) refers to as proactive and reactive countertransference. Proactive countertransference indicates what is in effect pathological material belonging to the counsellor which is introduced into the counselling relationship, whereas reactive countertransference refers to whatever it is in the counsellee to which the counsellor reacts. I offer below an example of proactive countertransference taken from a community work setting. Before leaving the point about proactive countertransference, I want to make the point that it is not useful to treat it as something dreadful which ought never to happen in well-regulated counselling circles. If the point about the pervasive nature of these phenomena is granted, then we must assume that all practitioners, no matter how conscientious and well supervised, will at some time do this. Proactive countertransference can even be helpful to the counsellee. Suppose, for example, the counsellor finds the counsellee extremely irritating, or attractive or frightening. We must assume that this says something about what the counsellor brings to the encounter. But we must also keep open the possibility that – in addition to that – the counsellee may, quite unawarely, be evoking these feelings in the counsellor. This is not a blame game about who does what first! (The same point holds true, of course, for the transference phenomenon. Experienced counsellors know that they tend to evoke certain sorts of transference in their counsellees and take that into account in their work and in supervision.) Once these feelings are explored, it is very often the case that important new learning can take place. Much of this countertransferential transaction is likely to be outside the awareness of both parties. This is one reason why pastoral counsellors increasingly acknowledge the importance of regular supervision of their work. A large part of the supervisor's task may lie in identifying transference and countertransference phenomena where they occur and especially where the counsellor is herself unaware of them. These supervisory interventions do not represent a negative criticism of the work but are understood as an integral component of the counselling process. As transference and countertransference are identified in supervision, so they can be taken back into the primary encounter between counsellor and counsellee to take forward their work.

In the context of a non-religious counselling service, the factors to which I have referred are, quite probably, operant. They may or may not constitute a large part of what happens. Let us consider an example. A worker in a community project is offering counselling to a young man who has severe financial problems. The work may be seen by both parties as a straightforward piece of debt counselling. The young man and the community worker may find that they work well together and reach some satisfactory conclusions. He plans his way forward and finds his depression lifts: she has the satisfaction of a job well done. They may not need to give any attention to their feelings (aware or unaware) for each other. Or it may be that the young man dismisses her as 'just like all social workers' (and other authority figures who try to prevent him living as he wishes – just like his mother does or did). The community worker may have to deal with the transference issues (and some countertransference too) in order to help the counsellee work out how he pushes away the help he seeks and, one hopes, how he can find ways to let older people support him when he needs it. Or it may be that the young man falls foul of some proactive countertransference by a stressed worker who, at a superficial level, is fed up with young people who drink and club away their funds and then expect her to pick up the pieces. If that anger is fed from a hidden source in her own history – perhaps bad memories of a father who drank his money and deprived and abused his family – it could be that the young man is in effect being punished for the sins of the counsellor's father.

Transference and countertransference in the work of the pastoral counsellor

Transference and countertransference are not confined to the consulting room or other place where the formal activity of counselling takes place. They are a part of everyday life and therefore, of course, part of the life of religious organisations and of those who make up such organisations. They are to be found in the context of pastoral counselling where the counsellor is identified with a religious organisation. However, there are also some complications which are unlikely to be found in the community project referred to above. It may be that the complications are greater because the religious matrix is simply different from a non-religious one, or it may be that the matrix of religion mobilises what Jung called 'archetypal transference'. In such an instance, in addition to the complications of transference and countertransference, there are the quasi-magical and other-worldly expectations which are not so much to do with the counsellee's expectations of another person but of whatever transcendent elements the counsellee associates with the counsellor or the counsellor's provenance (Clarkson 1995: 71–2).

Transference, as I have argued above, concerns fundamentally how we see others (and ourselves in relation to them) through the context of our early relationships. We also gain our earliest, foundational notions of God from our earliest relationships, and how we think of God subsequently is informed significantly by our early experiences. Those experiences are diverse, so that one person can have an impression of God as a persecutory person, derived from bad experiences of adults; or, through the mediation of other adults, of God as kind, loving and saving in contradistinction to some bad experiences. This is not to say that people are stuck for ever with their earliest perceptions of God – positive or negative. The relationship of transference and religious belief is reflexive. Thus, if we see God in terms of a negative father transference in our religious life, it may be that positive religious experience and teaching can undo some harmful effects and help to break down that tendency. A corollary might be a negative view of God taking the place of an earlier beneficent one. Such a negative view can arise from appalling experiences in later life. People speak of despair, a sense of God deserting them and abandoning them to a cruel fate. A woman, R, came for counselling on the suggestion of her doctor. She had been a deeply religious person brought up in the Jewish faith. She had been treated for depression, and her most depressed phases took the unusual form of barricading herself in her house, which she had stockpiled with food. At those times, she knew of a certainty that God had deserted her. If God existed, then he had ceased to care about his people. She was German in origin, but could not speak nor understand a word of that language. It transpired that she was a child survivor of one of the most notorious camps of the Third Reich. The 'Christians [had] killed [her] family like rats'. Small wonder that she refused to speak or understand the 'Christian' language, and a great wonder that she brought her grief, rage and despair to a counsellor associated with a church. In the work, she had to confront – through the person of the counsellor – the God who had so abandoned her and her family. No counsellee can do such work without great courage and no counsellor can bear the weight of such transference without compassionate support and supervision. The counsellee eventually recovered her mother tongue: it is unlikely she will remove the scars on her memory which, she felt, are all that keeps alive the memory of her dead.

There are other possibilities. For example, there are people who have less tendency to bring problematic transference phenomena into religious life and who can therefore offer useful critiques of oppressive religious experience and teaching to the benefit of others. Behind the multiple possibilities of early experience and views of God, there remains the constant of transference. What and how we transfer on to God is a powerful determinant of behaviour in and by religious groups. And, despite all theological differences, religious groups concur in their acknowledgement of the primacy of God and their dependence on God for life and sustenance. Bruce Reed (1978) makes the point that dependence and regression are intrinsic to the life of religious (in this case Christian) organisations. Reed's study was one carried out from a psychoanalytic and organisational viewpoint and carries with it corresponding values. It is possible to criticise his work as being too deterministic or even fatalistic in its view of human beings. One can advance theological criticisms about the inappropriateness of certain behaviours in the people of God who are called to be a royal priesthood. But Reed's argument rests upon an empirical and pragmatic view that everyone has their (quite proper) dependent needs. These may be met neurotically, and religious adherence or 'praxis' is certainly one way to do that. On the other hand, these basic needs may be handled more functionally and for the upbuilding or edification of those involved. For Reed, good religious practice entails an appropriate handling of dependent needs, most especially in worship, where we are all children of God and may, at times, properly (and temporarily) regress in that assured relationship.

That is not the same thing as saying that church congregations composed of adults should behave like dependent children, despite evidence that this does happen in many instances. Of particular interest for the pastoral worker, be she an ordained minister or a lay person charged with a counselling responsibility within or on behalf of the congregation, is the combination of a religious provenance with neurotic dependence on the part of the counsellee. In a religious context, there will be people seeking counselling who carry with them such a predisposition. It may be found in regular members of congregations and also in the population at large who make contact with a religious organisation (e.g. at a time of bereavement). The pastoral counsellor regularly meets these conditions, and her training should have equipped her to recognise the signs of such a transference. If we develop the example of working with a bereaved person, it is likely that the counsellor will be confronted with the pain of bereavement and will do her best to support the natural processes of grief and mourning, as well as paying attention to the bereft person's internal and external support systems, general health considerations and physical needs. In this respect the work will be quite like that of a counsellor in a secular agency.

The complications referred to above could emerge at any point in the counselling relationship. Pastoral counsellors commonly experience them in unkept appointments and avoidances. Sometimes they surface in more direct and challenging ways as when the bereft person turns on the counsellor (as in the example above) to blame her for the pain experienced. Startling though this can undoubtedly be, it is paradoxically often easier to encounter than the less aware or covert rejections and attacks because everything is out in the open. The counsellor knows she is not God and has no need to defend God. What the counsellor needs to be clear about at such times is that, although this attack is aimed at her and is intended to be as hurtful as it actually is, the real business is somewhere else. The 'God they ought to crucify' (Carter 1974: 29) is a God who should be explored by both parties in the counselling relationship. The counsellor will see very often that what ought to be crucified is the internalised image of an arbitrary and unloving parent who claims parental rights and privileges but who fails to give in turn appropriate love, respect and security. Part of the necessary working through transference would entail separating God and the counsellor and then confronting, rejecting, possibly even doing to death that unloving God. The work should in ideal circumstances not end there. The counsellor would have helped clear up some transference on to her and, quite possibly, might have exculpated God – on grounds of mistaken identity – from any responsibility for human suffering. There remains another layer of work for the counsellee and counsellor (but one beyond the scope of this chapter), which is to work out existentially how to hold God properly responsible. A God who is squeaky-clean in a dirty universe is – surely – not properly God. At such a point, counsellor and counsellee move beyond the transference relationship and into a person-to-person or 'real' relationship (Clarkson, 1995: 13–18; 146ff) of joint exploration of ultimate mysteries.

One final example, this time of a positive transference. From Freud's time onwards, it has been noted that one of the most common forms of transference is the positive transference, and this is nowhere more true than in pastoral counselling. In the *Introductory Lecture* cited earlier, Freud spoke to his audience about how some patients gave him and his colleagues the distinct impression that they could be cured only by love and that they had found in this therapeutic relationship the very thing they sought. Freud warned of the danger that the analyst might be beguiled into believing the publicity about himself. The same warning should be offered to every pastoral counsellor. She or he may be identified as not only the most lovable and loving person to undertake this great work but quite possibly as one uniquely endowed with the spirit of the Christ or some other salvific person. Such a counsellor is someone one wants to please and whose smile is enough gratification to get one through a tough week. The warning is simple: believe it, and you are lost. The next step is most likely to be a catastrophic movement into negative transference. I do not claim to have done the mathematical work here, but I am struck by the aptness of Christopher Zeeman's catastrophe theory as applied, for instance, to stress behaviour in prison populations or crowd behaviour. Catastrophe theory as applied to human behaviour is modelled on the behaviour of plane metal surfaces subjected to certain stresses. As the stresses build they reach a cusp, at which point, the least little change will precipitate a crisis out of all proportion to the immediate stress, the point of catastrophe (Zeeman 1977). The risk of catastrophic reversal does not mean that positive transference can have no functionally positive value. Recognised and dealt with openly, it can lead into an understanding of the barely articulable longings of the counsellee. His dreams may not come true that way, but he is likely to end up with a greater capacity for intimacy in his own life if he can integrate that material into his important relationships.

This is indeed more charged than those situations where the client has no evidence of the religious or other background of the counsellor. It has to be said, however, that there are probably very few situations where the counsellee actually knows nothing about the person of the counsellor. Even where great emphasis is placed upon not disclosing any information, counsellees become adept at cracking the codes employed by practitioners, secretaries and receptionists! The identification between the counsellor and God need not be a crude one: it could be subtle and subliminal in, for example, identifying the counsellor and the Christ. Unfortunately, much religious practice tends to reinforce these identifications. Consider, for instance, the anomalous identifications which might take place in the most psychologically robust people who, week after week, experience their pastoral counsellor standing six feet above contradiction in a pulpit claiming authority to speak the word of God. Or consider what it must be like to see your counsellor presiding at a table where is served the Body and Blood of Christ. These stark examples are adduced to show how the fact of a religious provenance is likely to be most strongly suggestive in the case of ordained people, which is why there is a debate to be had about the appropriateness of ministers having counselling relationships within their own congregations (Lyall 1995).

It is not helpful for those who hold a high doctrine of ordination to assert that this association can have powerful healing effects. These may exist and they may lie at the heart of much folk religion and shamanism. They do not, however, go well in the context of pastoral counselling as understood and practised in modern cultures, except insofar as they provide material to be deconstructed on the way to healing. Furthermore, such arguments sometimes mask unaware countertransferences. Ministers may be aware of the 'strokes' that come from exercising the role of trusted pastor: they may not be so aware of the flip side, which is the tendency to view lay members of the church as weaker than themselves and in need of their pastoral care. This is an example of proactive countertransference and is likely to lead to exits on the part of the healthy and an increase in neurotic dependence on the part of more needy people. Evidence of the widespread nature of this countertransference may be found in correspondence columns in church newspapers and conversation at ministerial gatherings, where such attitudes may be rehearsed as though they were virtues. Many more aware ordained people will admit to discovering something of this in themselves.

This is not a new problem. Anthony Russell pointed out in 1980 that the clerical profession in one sense predates professions, but that in the nineteenth century clerics became 'anxious to regard themselves and be regarded by society as a professional body with specific functions and duties' (Russell 1980: 6). The many roles Russell studies include that of pastor as well as catechist, clerk, officer of law and order, almoner, teacher, officer of health and politician. All this on top of being a preacher and leader of public worship! Russell's view is that of a sociologist who is also an ordained minister. Much earlier in this century, a non-sociological but equally pragmatic approach was taken by Roland Allen (1960) who maintained that it was an inappropriate regard for the ordained ministry that was killing the liveliness of the Church. This was not because of stupidity or malignity on the part of the clergy. He was studying the Church in India and noted how the mother Church sent her brightest and best to serve in India. Allen did not write in terms of transference, but he pointed out that what was killing the Church was the way in which the clergy were (inappropriately) respected and deferred to

105

– as though local Christians were not far better placed to be ministers of the gospel.

We cannot go back beyond Russell and Allen and ask of, say, medieval people how they dealt with transference issues because those issues are themselves a cultural product of the modern and postmodern periods. Perhaps all we can do is to acknowledge that, whatever the benefits of designated religious leaders, there is a downside which can best be understood as tending to support transference and inappropriate types of dependence (and countertransference). In the pastoral context, counsellors aim to help people become more autonomous, resourceful and able to deal with life's difficulties out of their own resources, including the resources of the religious message or Gospel as lived and experienced in communities. Whatever hampers them in this task deserves critical scrutiny. After all, if certain features of ecclesial life make pastoral counselling difficult for those who are troubled, then those people may be assumed to be the acute tip of a chronic iceberg which perhaps represents a large percentage of the rest of the religious and secular community. This is not merely an emotional and mental health consideration, important though that is, but an indicator of a missionary or evangelistic task which lies all around.

REFERENCES

Allen, R. (1960) *Missionary Methods: St. Paul's or Ours?* London: World Dominion Books.

Carter, S. (1974) *Green Print for Song*, London: Stainer & Bell.

Clarkson, P. (1995) *The Therapeutic Relationship in Psychoanalysis, Counselling Psychology and Psychotherapy*, London: Whurr.

Freud, S. (1917/1991) 'General theory of the neuroses, Lecture 27: Transference', in *Introductory Lectures on Psychoanalysis* (vol. 1, *Penguin Freud Library*), London: Penguin.

Laplanche, J. and Pontalis, J.B. (1988) *The Language of Psycho-analysis* (trans. D. Nicholson-Smith), London: Karnac.

Lyall, D. (1995) *Counselling in the Pastoral and Spiritual Context*, Buckingham: Open University Press.

Reed, B. (1978) *The Dynamics of Religion: Process and Movement in Christian Churches*, London: Darton, Longman & Todd.

Russell, A. (1980). *The Clerical Profession*, London: SPCK.

Wolf, E.S. (1988) *Treating the Self: Elements of Clinical Self Psychology*, New York: Guilford Press.

Zeeman, E.C. (1977) *Catastrophe Theory: Selected Papers, 1972–1977*, London: Addison-Wesley.

8

PASTORAL COUNSELLING WITH THOSE WHO HAVE EXPERIENCED ABUSE IN RELIGIOUS SETTINGS

Ruth Layzell

Introduction

When I was sorting through some bookshelves recently, I rediscovered a book of cartoons (Portlock 1990) depicting the absurd side of church life. One of them caught my eye. In it, a stern-looking little boy is addressing his rather alarmed, newspaper-reading, middle-aged father. The caption runs: 'God told me last night if you didn't buy me a bike before summer, he'd make you go bald.' The cartoon is funny not only because of its absurdity, but also because it carries with it a grain of truth. The humour exposes the (mostly hidden and unacknowledged) potential in religious people to use their spirituality or their religious practice as an offensive weapon, seeking out a vulnerable spot in another person (in this case fear of baldness) to serve their own interests (getting a bike).

Most spiritual abuse is not as blatant or obvious as our small boy's statement. It is more subtle and pernicious, often appearing upright, blameless or godly to the uninformed observer, yet carrying with it the potential to devastate those on the receiving end. Its hiddenness is one of the difficult things about it. But this potential for abuse to take place in religious contexts is beginning to be uncovered. Communities of faith face a challenge to examine their theology, structures and religious practices with a more constructively critical eye than has been the case in the past, when the assumption has often been that 'abuse cannot happen here' because we are serving God.

Another challenge is to those of us who work as pastoral counsellors. Although some survivors of abuse in a religious context will be utterly alienated from people of faith, others will want to seek understanding and healing in the company of someone who understands 'from the inside'. Yet such people may be hard to find because abusive behaviour depends on the compliance and silence of the person who is abused. Survivors will need a safe person and a safe place away from the immediate network – perhaps the very context of the abuse – where the abusive experience can be recognised for what it is. Pastoral counsellors are likely to be called upon as those who can hear the stories of religious abuse which cannot easily be voiced elsewhere. The challenge for us as practitioners is so to recognise and understand religious or spiritual abuse that the work done in the counselling room may lead to the healing and restoration which the client seeks.

In this chapter, then, I shall define the nature of religious abuse; explore the climate in which it may occur; describe the experience and effects of abuse; and outline the therapeutic task for counsellors working with survivors.

One disclaimer before I begin. In an age of religious pluralism, it is difficult to discuss the abusive aspects of religion without reference to the different religious cultures which make up our present society. But I have chosen here to look at the topic from the particularity of my own point of view in order to be specific and clear in articulating my observations. I therefore make no apology for speaking as a Christian, with experience of non-conformism, through my Baptist upbringing, and of Anglicanism, through my involvement in evangelical, Anglo-Catholic and charismatic parishes. Where I talk about abuse in religious settings, it is in these contexts that I have encountered it, both in my own and in my friends' and clients' experiences. I suspect that much of what I have to say may also be true of other faith communities and settings, but it will be for others to draw the parallels and make the links into their own situation.

Abuse in religious contexts

Like others who have explored the area of abusive behaviour in the context of religion, I take the view that such abuse constitutes a misuse of power (see Rutter 1989: 48; Poling 1991: 23; Walker 1997: 5–9). The most obvious definition of power is simply that it is the energy that enables us to be and to act. 'Power is co-extensive with life itself . . . to be alive is to exercise power in some degree' (Loomer 1976: 12). The Bible talks of this energy of life as being brought into existence and sustained by God, who declares that the created order is good. In addition, God gives human beings the power not only to exist, but also to act – to name, to nurture and to wield authority (Genesis 1, 2). Power for human beings is thus also 'the ability to act in effective ways with the objects and people that make up our . . . world' (Poling 1991: 24).

Defined in these ways, power is something we all have to some degree. It is not something which some people exercise and others suffer, but it is experienced in relationship as an interplay of energies:

> Power is often misunderstood as a one-way effect on others. But power is actually organised by the relational webs of which we are part. Our ability to act depends on our connections with other persons and with the institutions and ideas that form the basis of our experience.
>
> (Poling 1991: 24)

This implies that in relationship with each other, human beings have the power to enhance or limit each other's enjoyment of the creative potential of life, whether or not we see ourselves as powerful. For example, when my children are behaving well, I can be 'kind mummy' (which is an image I enjoy). When they behave badly, I become 'angry mummy' (an image I do not particularly enjoy). Although I hold the balance of power, they nonetheless have sufficient power to affect and influence how I behave and even how I experience myself.

However, if everyone who is alive has power, it is certainly true that some have more power than others. As human beings, we organise ourselves socially so that some people relinquish certain sorts of power and others assume it so that things which we need get done. And as life unfolds, there are times when we are powerful and other times when we are vulnerable and dependent on others.

I suspect that almost universally we find it easier to feel powerful than to feel needy, yet these experiences of vulnerability are necessary to us if we are to live a full life. We cannot encounter a new experience or master a new skill without accepting the vulnerability of not knowing. We cannot be intimate with another without the vulnerability of dismantling our defences and making ourselves known. We cannot articulate our deepest hopes and longings without unmasking ourselves, cannot be cared for or helped without acknowledging our needs.

Yet our times of vulnerability represent not only great opportunity for us in this way, but also great risk. For at such times, as we depend on another intellectually, emotionally or physically, we also depend on them spiritually. We have to trust to the goodness of another if we ourselves are to grow; we open to them some aspect of our identity – the part of us which is waiting for birth; and we place our hope in their hands as we look forward to what may come to be. All these things – trust, identity, hope – are at the same time precious and precarious, fragile yet of ultimate importance. They are the qualities which make our life creative, open and worth living and without which we are diminished, hemmed in and prey to despair.

In these moments of great risk, the outcome for us is largely not in our hands, but in the hands of those who have power in relation to us:

> The power of the individual is enhanced when the web of relationships is benevolent and encourages the most creativity. . . . Relational power for the individual person as just described depends on a just and creative social environment.
>
> (Poling 1991: 25–6)

Whether or not we realise the potential of this creative vulnerability depends on the choice of another person, either to benefit us or to benefit themselves. The choice they make will either enhance or undermine our sense of self, our ability to trust and our ground for hope. As Rutter puts it:

> How a woman is treated in relationships of trust can make the difference between whether she experiences her femininity as a force to be valued and respected or as a commodity to be exploited. Sexual violation of the forbidden zone can kill off hope itself.
>
> (1989: 30)

The same is true of any other aspect of our selves which we entrust to the care of another. So, for example, how a child is treated by those who care for her will make the difference between whether she experiences her vulnerability and dependence as a quality to be cherished and respected or to be cut off and despised.

Because of the human potential to behave opportunistically, it is this 'just and creative social environment' which is enjoined in the biblical concept of covenant (and which we also see in counselling contracts and codes of ethics). Covenant allows vulnerability to be safely present in relationship, by requiring the commitment of that which is strong to the protection of that which is vulnerable. In some relationships, vulnerability and strength are present for both parties in fairly equal measure. But in others (e.g. parents/children, teachers/pupils, counsellors/clients, clergy/parishioners), power is biased in one direction. Rutter (1989: 30) says that such power is conferred 'as part of an ancient moral bargain' in which the person with power 'holds a sacred trust' to guard the welfare of the other until what is vulnerable has grown into strength.

But to act in the way Rutter describes requires a degree of risk, which not everyone can manage. 'We are created for communion with God and our neighbour . . . on terms which require courage and trust in a future we cannot see, which postpones fulfilment and does not allow every kind of immediate gratification' (Williams 1968: 153). In order to commit our strength to the protection of that which is vulnerable, we must believe, first, that we actually are strong; second, that we will not be destroyed by acting in the interests of another; and third, that the effort is worthwhile.

To be in relationship with another, even from a position of strength, and to care about their well-being in any real way, is, paradoxically, to make oneself vulnerable and to give away power. In order to take this risk, a person must have the sense that they are secure and strong enough to cope with it and that any denial of what they want in the service of another is more important than their own immediate gratification. If those in positions of power do not experience themselves as powerful, they will have little idea that they are capable of defending anything, let alone the vulnerability of another person. Indeed, they may experience themselves as the vulnerable one in need of protection. If, in addition, they have learned to mistrust others, they may well fear that to give anything away will be to risk being damaged or annihilated. Rather than take the risk, they choose to stay in control and limit the possibility of real relationship and real growth for the other. Thus, as Poling comments:

> [The] abuse of power for the individual is motivated by fear and by the resulting desire to control the power of life. . . . The power that is intended by God for everyone who lives is used to destroy relationships in exchange for control. Rather than live in insecurity, some persons choose to create structures that dominate and control others for personal gratification and false security.
>
> (1991: 27)

Abuse, then, is a violation of covenant, the 'sacred trust' to protect vulnerability. It occurs when those in power exploit the vulnerability of those in their care in order to further their vested interest. And, whatever form it takes (emotional, physical, sexual), abuse always has spiritual consequences.

The abuser is diminished by his choice to try to control and dominate not only the vulnerable person, but also the very power of life itself. It is a choice for self and death rather than a choice in favour of love and life. 'It is the way of the Devil, who wants to become God; it is the abuse of others for self-glorification or self-gratification; it is the way of fallen humanity that would lord it over others if only they could' (Walker 1997: 5–6).

The abused person also sustains a spiritual wound. The trust and hope which they had invested in the abuser turns out to be ill placed and the fragile sense of identity, which looked to the other for validation, is damaged. Their access to the creative power of life is diminished and various forms of psychological self-defence are needed in order to survive. Perhaps the deepest wounds are sustained in the messages: 'You do not matter,' 'You have no intrinsic value,' 'You are not loved.'

If all abuse has spiritual consequences, is there anything particular to be said about abuse in religious contexts? I believe so. First, I want to suggest that when a person is in a place of spiritual searching, she makes the deepest parts of herself vulnerable. To be wounded in these places is a very serious matter. Further, if, as I believe, God is the giver and sustainer of life, whose nature (seen supremely in the person and life of Christ) is love, to discover abuse among those who claim to follow him threatens and distorts fundamental and vital truth. For the messages of abuse ('you do not matter,' 'you have no intrinsic value,' 'you are not loved') run directly counter to the message of the Gospel ('you are loved so much that God has given all he has for you').

Abuse in a religious context, then, constitutes a double blow to the spirit – the first as the result of abuse and the second in that where a person might reasonably have expected to find love and hope and life, what they experience is death-dealing and hope-destroying. It is no accident that Jesus' harshest words (Matthew 23) are addressed to religious leaders. Abuse in a religious setting is such a distortion of the creative potential given to humanity by God that it can appropriately be described as evil.

The context of abuse in religious settings

It seems so obvious that those who have responsibility for the spiritual welfare of others should take care to nurture and not injure them that it may strike us as almost inconceivable that spiritual abuse can happen. Yet, I know from friends, clients and from my own experience that it does. So what factors come into play to produce abuse in religious settings and so deal the double blow to the spirit which I have described?

Walker (1997: 6) comments that it is rare that religious abuse is 'deliberately orchestrated by unscrupulous persons'. 'More typically,' he says, 'it results from well-meaning, misguided or deluded authority figures; or simply through the unreflective practice of sedimented traditions and conventional wisdom.' Similarly, Poling (1991: 31) notes that abuse can happen in 'blind zones' created by communities where 'certain relationship systems are regarded as normative and therefore not open to scrutiny', and where communities protect such systems from criticism because of their own need to idealise them. If we are to be able to hear the stories of those who have experienced abuse, we need to open our eyes to the dynamics which allow it to lurk in our midst.

One of the ways in which we express a longing for a fuller life is to project onto certain individuals or groups the qualities which we want for ourselves. Communities of faith often carry people's hopes for safety, nurture and significance which stem from the wounds of childhood ('my own family did not understand me, nurture me or keep me safe, but here I will find kind and loving people who will'). There is something appropriate about this, because such communities should reflect the nature of the God they serve. But when the need for these things is deep or urgent, the temptation is to idealise, creating the illusion of perfection in the present by suppressing or denying those parts of experience which do not fit the image.

This sets the scene for what has been called 'a state of delusional equilibrium' where we keep things 'calm and smooth on the top [so that] the chaos just beneath the surface need not be addressed' (Robinson 1996). The trouble is that when unwelcome reality does intrude, you have to 'find a scapegoat – someone you can vilify, character assassinate and expel as a corporate common enemy', in order to be able to return to the state of delusional equilibrium.

Here we have two of the dynamics which make abuse in a religious context possible. The first is that what is not part of the illusory image cannot be seen. This means that either those suffering know instinctively that it will be futile to speak of their experience or, if they do speak, the community goes into denial rather than allow any challenge to their ideal:

> When [abuse] occurs within an environment of taboo and silence, the experience of victims is excluded from the concern of the community. Victims are marginal as persons because the suffering of their lives has to be suppressed.
>
> (Poling 1991: 148)

Victims of abuse are therefore implicitly told to keep their silence.

Melanie, the daughter of a churchwarden and the wife of an ordinand, became aware during counselling that her father had sexually abused her as a child. Appalled by the implications of such memories, she talked with her sisters, whose experience confirmed hers. When the vicar of their parents' church heard of the crisis, he visited the parents, who together protested Melanie's father's innocence. The vicar then took the view that the daughters should be reconciled to their parents (without any acknowledgement that their father had wronged them) so as not to cause further distress and 'split the church'. Because Melanie's parents would not discuss their memories, it became impossible for the daughters to maintain normal family relationships and the family, rather than the church, was split. In addition, Melanie and her husband were cut off from the support of their home church, as it was impossible for them to go back. The vicar had protected the church community, but had effectively expelled the victim, thereby compounding the abuse.

The second dynamic is when an individual comes to represent or focus the malaise in a community. A number of the stories I have heard have testified to this. Because of who they were – female, pastorally sensitive, lay people, gay, vulnerable – or because of what they were noticing in the community, they became convenient scapegoats. This is exemplified in the following stories.

Martin was part-way through training for the ministry when he finally acknowledged his gay sexuality. With great integrity, and at considerable cost to himself, he discussed the matter with his sponsoring diocese, which initiated a long, personally intrusive process whose aim was never clear. His training was suspended and he eventually deduced that the bishop would not ordain him even though he was not in a relationship. For some time after he finally withdrew from training, Martin found churchgoing extremely painful.

Jane is an intellectually very able woman, with strong pastoral gifts, who was ordained not long after women were admitted to the Anglican priesthood. Her curacy, with a man whose reputation as a training incumbent was good and who declared himself content to work with women, promised much in her development as a minister. The reality, however, was very different. Jane found him to be distant and cold, prescriptive about what she should do and intolerant of her having different ideas (about pastoral work especially). He gave her no opportunity to discuss her difficulties or uncertainties with him and the only feedback he gave her was when she did something he did not like. Then he would correct her. He forbade or undermined her attempts to find fellowship and support in her new ministry and she ended up overworking to prove to herself that she was doing well. After months of struggling, Jane was signed off because of overwork and stress and eventually had to leave the parish.

These two stories show the scapegoating dynamic in action. In a Church which has not decided how to respond to gay people and has not really come to terms with admitting women to positions of authority, we wish the 'problem' would go away. Because it is not acceptable to admit that there is a problem, we punish those who focus it until it is impossible for them to stay. Those in power are relieved, but the vulnerable individual ends up bearing the pain of the tension on behalf of the community. The trouble with this way of resolving tensions, however, is that the dynamic is infinitely repeatable (together with the resulting abuse) until the underlying issues are faced.

Naïvety is another problem. When people are operating from the unscriptural assumption that the kingdom of God has come in its fullness in the form of the Church, it is easy to assume that everything which happens inside the Church is good. This may lead to a naïvety about the potential for harm ('because we mean well, we cannot do ill', Hunt 1997: 60), and a lack of critical appraisal of what we do (Tomlinson 1997: 39). This can, at one end of the spectrum, lead to uninformed pastoral practice in which we think that we have nothing to learn from the insights of the personal and social sciences, or, at the other, to abuse.

If abuse is the exploitation of vulnerability by the powerful for their own ends, those ministries (such as healing and deliverance) which focus on the vulnerability of those prayed with and the expertise of those who pray are most likely to become abusive (Tomlinson 1997: 38). We may not be talking here about the gross abuse of physical harm or sexual exploitation, but about any opportunistic use of a person's vulnerability to manipulate a result, push a point or get one up on another person.

For example, Sarah, a member of the church leadership team, distressed by her infertility, went for prayer after the service on Mothering Sunday and the other person praying for her took the opportunity to explain to Sarah the ways in which her lifestyle and career probably prevent conception. This exploitation of another's vulnerability is abusive. Or when Tanya, a young teenager, who secretly believes she was the cause of her parents' divorce and is driven by a desire to atone, understands that what is expected when she is prayed with at a charismatic meeting is that she fall down, she does so. She has pleased the people she went with (who feel there has been a success in their ministry) but goes home feeling empty. Unwittingly, because they have not taken time to get to know her, those who prayed with her have exploited her vulnerability for the sake of their success.

All the dynamics described above have at their root a dualistic split which equates 'spiritual' with goodness and 'material' with evil. This position can be taken further so that 'church' (our church, usually) is seen as good and 'world' is seen as bad. Then nothing inside the church can be criticised while everything outside the church is to be mistrusted. Such a belief forms the basis for another kind of religious abusive practice. In this view, bad flesh – our physical, material experience – must be 'mastered' so that good spirit can grow. What happens to the body is then of no consequence so long as spiritual purity is the aim, and love is defined as the effort of the parent or pastor to purify the spirit by subduing the flesh. Miller (1987: 3–91) and Rubin (1997: 81–98) describe how theologies that encourage conversion as a pilgrimage of self-annihilation of the 'natural man', and a lifelong inner warfare against indwelling sin, can be used to justify all kinds of physical and emotional abuse, with devastating results in the life of the believer. When the word 'love' is associated with experiences of harm and when those who express such 'love' are seen to be God's representatives, the survivor may struggle with guilt, anger, anxiety over salvation, an inability to act or decide for herself or lack of confidence in doing so.

Another case story illustrates this point. Joshua, a vicarage child, continues to live with the confusion generated by his upbringing. His father, who was perceived by others to be a marvellous vicar, was never there for him, always working and never saying no to any other person's requests for his help. His mother, left to bring up four boisterous children alone, and terrified that they would 'go astray', expressed her fear by beating the children, two of whom were seriously injured as a result of her violence. Alongside the absence of his father and the intrusive presence of his mother, Joshua was assured that both his parents and the God they served loved him. As an adult, Joshua belongs to a church but is highly mistrustful of a God of love.

In all these stories, there are common strands. In each, abuse has found and exploited some area of vulnerability, from the dependence of childhood and apprenticeship to the openness of those seeking the touch of God in their lives through prayer ministry. But abuse is hidden; either by the standing of the abuser or by a rationale which sounds all right but is experienced as all wrong. The hiddenness of the abuse (which may be emphasised by the isolation of the abused person) means that the silence of the victim is almost guaranteed. Lastly, in each situation instead of finding welcome, healing and support, the experience leaves the abused person confused, angry, disabled or shamed. In each case, far from helping them on their spiritual journey, they end up with more difficulty in relation to God and religion than they had before.

In each situation, some form of dehumanising has taken place. A system of ideas, a universalised ministry technique, one's own status or comfort becomes more important than response to a person. In some situations, the vulnerable person may have been compartmentalised and dealt with as if one part of their person can be touched without affecting the whole. In others, the abuser may believe he has a right (even a divine right) to dominance over another (e.g. men over women, adults over children) and this takes precedence over any imperative to care for them.

Perhaps the most devastating combination is where a child has been brought up in a way which has left them wounded or confused, and then experiences further abuse as an adult. The compulsion to repeat what is unresolved means they are likely to put themselves somewhere where they can attend to what they lacked in childhood. The hope is that they may find healing; the risk is that they leave themselves vulnerable to being wounded again. All too often what they find is a church which lacks both the health and the awareness to make a difference. They are easy prey for the unscrupulous, but the unhealed wounds are sore spots which can be rubbed raw by the lack of awareness or the abusive practice of those who should have a greater care.

The therapeutic task

We have seen that because human beings develop in the context of their relationships, abuse – especially in religious contexts – has real and far-reaching consequences for their spiritual well-being. But it is this very sensitivity to the influence of others in relationship which also provides the ground for hope in the therapeutic process. If the spirit of a person can be damaged by the abusive or ill-informed actions of others, that same spirit may be soothed, healed or enabled to grow through careful, respectful and well-informed relationship.

If, as I have argued, abuse is the exploitation by those in power of the vulnerability of those in their care, then the survivor shows a remarkable degree of courage in coming to counselling at all. The counsellor must demonstrate, by being reliable, trustworthy and congruent in the relationship, the care for the client's vulnerability which she did not experience in the abusive environment. This was the experience of Karen, a survivor of abuse in a religious setting:

> I was able to respond to their caring because I sensed they would not hurt me. They believed me, listened to me, and I, being so hungry for someone to hear me began to believe they had my best interests at heart. When someone cared enough to attend to me, I risked reaching out.
>
> (Poling 1991: 45–6)

But such reaching out is a risk, and some degree of mistrust and resistance is likely. Resistance may be more marked in relation to a pastoral counsellor if the abuse has taken place in a religious context. Some of the mechanisms the client chooses (e.g. not going to church, not praying, being angry with God, refusing to be prayed with, throwing out faith altogether) may not be readily understood by her faith community. She may even have experienced further abuse as people have tried to pray the problem away or told her that her behaviour jeopardises her eternal salvation. It is vital that the counsellor respects what the client does to keep herself safe, both within and outside the counselling relationship, and welcomes this as a hopeful sign of her determination to be well.

I want to suggest that once the parameters are established, the heart of the work is simple in essence – though complex in practice. It is to enable the client to recover, to articulate and to integrate their story. Michael Williams describes how the activity of 'writing our own story' is a central part of being human:

To live is to 'write' my own biography. I gather, select and sift through all the internal and external events of my life and I 'write' the story that becomes me. In some respects I have great freedom in this writing, in other respects I have little option but to include that which I would rather not. Sometimes I can choose what to include and how to frame it. At other times, others try to force me to frame things according to their criteria. They attempt to possess me, to violate me, to rape me. Sometimes they succeed. When my story is simply the stories that I have been given by others then I cease to be. To have a story is not sufficient. I must have a hand in writing it to be human.

(1997: 27–8)

The converse of this, of course, is that attempts on the part of others to dictate the story, which should be my own, are dehumanising and reduce my capacity to be fully myself, no matter how benign their motivation. Perhaps some of Princess Diana's appeal, particularly for women and marginal groups, was that she exemplified a refusal to be defined (limited) by a script she had not chosen, and that she found ways of speaking with her own voice against what she felt to be overwhelming odds.

Survivors of abuse will have experienced the violation Williams describes in other people's attempts to write their story for them. Yet in coming for counselling at all, they will already have found within themselves some reserves of courage to refuse or resist this dehumanisation. What they need, therefore, is a welcoming, hospitable space in which their story – their version of events, their hopes and aspirations – can be heard without being censored or edited.

However, being able to speak at all may be a monumental task given that abuse silences the victim. The abused person's first task, then, is to overcome the conditions or mechanisms which maintained her silence, find her voice and be able to articulate her experience. If the abuse began in childhood and especially if it has been reinforced by subsequent experience, such speech may seem almost impossible. Only people who exist have a voice. Those who have been made to feel that they are nothing may struggle to become articulate. The client will need to establish, through the counsellor's attentive presence, enough sense of self to feel that they have something to say. If shaming and fear have achieved the silence, the client will need to experience enough respect and safety in the relationship to be able to speak. In order for the client to find her voice, the counsellor's task will be to convey: 'I believe you are somebody,' 'I want to hear you,' 'I value you,' 'it's safe to speak here.'

Using our voice is one of the earliest ways in which we affect our environment and so it is one of the most primitive forms of personal potency. A baby soon learns that adults will respond to his cry, and when language is mastered, the ability to 'gather, select and sift through' the events of our life and 'write' our story (Williams 1997) is significantly enhanced. We not only shape our own experience, but can influence others by what we say. Being unable to speak about experiences of abuse is therefore to lose some measure of potency and control. To quote again from the words of Karen:

> My greatest victory has been to break the promise and tell my story. I have been able to use the power of writing and speech to transform, to change anger, fear, shame, and guilt into useful tools for cutting away lies and deception.
>
> (Poling 1991: 41)

To name something is to gain purchase on it, and Karen experienced the power of words as they transformed the very feelings which had disabled her into tools to set her free. Describing an experience for myself is to articulate my story, even if it contains elements I did not want. As I describe it, I can at least choose how to respond to it and so add elements which are distinctively mine. As the counsellor gives her client space to tell her story in her own way, so she begins to address the erosion of potency and control implicit in abuse, giving her client freedom to choose, decide, interpret and shape the story as it continues.

As we have seen, in order for one person to abuse another they must dehumanise them in some way. This means that being misunderstood or negated by a significant other will be part of the experience for the abused person. As Josselson (1996: 108) comments, 'Not to be understood [is] tantamount to ceasing to exist, to the destruction of the self.' It is this lack of validation which may make it difficult for a survivor of abuse to 'realise' their experience:

> By becoming real to another we become real to ourselves. Eye-to-eye contact with a responsive other gives us confidence in our own experience, allows us to feel . . . and shapes what we come to believe about ourselves.
>
> (Josselson 1996: 101)

Until another person has confirmed what I feel, I do not know whether it is real or only in my head, whether it is reasonable or crazy. But when I see sadness or pain in another's eyes as I recount my story, I can recognise that what I have experienced really is sad or painful. Such empathy from the counsellor gives the client – perhaps for the first time – the opportunity to become real to herself and to learn that her own perceptions and interpretations can be trusted.

But the counsellor's empathic response may be complex for the client. If the abuser's denial, the collusion of bystanders, injunctions 'not to be angry but to forgive', and the abused person's own need to survive conspire to mask the full weight of an experience of abuse, the counsellor's empathy is likely to unmask it. This is vital for the survivor, for, to heal, she needs to know both that she has been wounded and how extensive the wound is. So 'she must allow the defensive structure of denial and dissociation to fall apart' (Poling 1991: 115) and feel the pain of the abuse in order to recognise the truth and allow the wound to be tended. This part of the journey is paradoxical. Rather than feeling better, the client is likely to feel worse. This point is again illustrated in the experience of Karen:

> When she let down her guard Karen ... became ill and discovered that she could not survive unless she faced the truth of her life which threatened to break her spirit. . . . She had to face waves of grief and suffering about her life, which often seemed more than she could bear.
>
> (Poling 1991: 115–16)

Feeling the pain will include allowing anger and bitterness to surface:

> If I can feel outrage at the injustice I have suffered, can recognise my persecution as such, and can acknowledge and hate my persecutor for what he or she has done, only then ... will the repressed anger, rage and hatred cease to be perpetuated.
>
> (Miller 1987: 248)

This is a process for the survivor of refusing any longer to bear the cost of the abuse in herself, putting the responsibility appropriately with the abuser and sluicing out its toxic effect on herself.

The final part of the client's journey of healing is to recover a sense of identity which integrates but is not confined by the abuse. To do this, she must step outside the frame of reference – that 'desire to control the power of life' (Poling 1991: 27) – which led to her abuse, into something beyond her current experience. Here we hit another paradox. For, having regained some sense of control, this step involves letting go of it again:

Once I stopped fighting the story . . . I surrendered my need
to control my creation and liberation, and allowed myself to
follow. . . . It was a member of my support group who finally
convinced me that I could survive if I gave up the need to
control my journey.

(Karen in Poling 1991: 45)

Survivors use the language of birth, creation, or seismic change to
describe the moment because it is like emerging into a completely
different landscape. In Karen's words:

My moment of transformation was like the story in Genesis.
Creation occurred following the time of nothingness. Out of
chaos came the new, the fresh.

(Poling 1991: 45)

Such a step involves surrendering control and choosing to live with
insecurity, vulnerability and risk. It means relinquishing the desire for
vengeance in order to forgive, replacing hate with love, living hopefully
and generously, by faith and trust.

In Christian terms, to do this is to allow my story to connect
with the Big Story – God's story. Indeed, despite the truth-distorting
experience of abuse, somewhere the survivor holds a stubborn faith that
things could be otherwise and, where such faith is strained to or beyond
its limits, the pastoral counsellor may hold it for and with her. Faith – in
a God who welcomes and does not attempt to control me; who wants to
hear my voice; who is tender with my suffering and wants me to be well;
who is angered at the wrong done to me and stands between me and my
abuser with justice and with mercy; who brings life even out of death;
and who calls me to share this risky, creative life with him – resources
and contains the journey of healing which the survivor undertakes and
the work of the counsellor who accompanies her. It is God's story which
provides the ground for hope and a model for the new way of living
which is open to her at the moment of surrender:

We come to the deepest mystery when we see in the suffering
of Jesus a disclosure of the love of God. . . . What Jesus reveals
on the cross . . . is the love which does not shirk suffering, and
that love is God himself at work. . . . The cause of Jesus'
suffering is sin and the human predicament. He meets the
situation by bearing what has to be borne that the work of love

may get done. God in Jesus Christ suffers with his world, not meaninglessly, but redemptively. He has inaugurated a new history by an action which restores the possibility of loyalty in this broken, suffering, yet still hopeful human community.

(Williams 1968: 185–6)

REFERENCES

Hunt, S. (1997) 'Giving the Devil more than his due', in L. Osborn and A. Walker (eds), *Harmful Religion*, London: SPCK, 43–64.

Josselson, R. (1996) *The Space Between Us*, Thousand Oaks: Sage.

Loomer, B. (1976) 'Two conceptions of power', *Criterion*, 15: 12.

Miller, A. (1987) *For Your Own Good*, London: Virago.

Poling, J.N. (1991) *The Abuse of Power: A Theological Problem*, Nashville: Abingdon.

Portlock, R. (1990) *Way Off the Church Wall*, London: Marshall Pickering.

Robinson, W. (1996) 'United but not confused; distinct but not separate', unpublished lecture, *Continuing the Journey*, Swanwick.

Rubin, J. (1997) 'The other side of joy', in L. Osborn and A. Walker (eds), *Harmful Religion*, London: SPCK, 81–98.

Rutter, P. (1989) *Sex in the Forbidden Zone*, London: Mandala.

Tomlinson, D. (1997) 'Shepherding: care or control?', in L. Osborn and A. Walker (eds), *Harmful Religion*, London: SPCK, 26–42.

Walker, A. (1997) 'Exploring harmful religion', in L. Osborn and A. Walker (eds), *Harmful Religion*, London: SPCK, 1–11.

Williams, D. (1968) *The Spirit and the Forms of Love*, New York: Harper & Row.

Williams, M. (1997) 'Tragedy and pastoral care', *Contact*, 123: 26–31.

9

THE CHALLENGE AND PROMISE OF PASTORAL COUNSELLING

John Foskett

Introduction

At the European conference on pastoral care and counselling held in Ripon in 1997 two themes emerged, as if from hiding.[1] First was the theme of marginalisation. The conference opened with two women rabbis leading us in Shabatt, the keeping of the Sabbath, and ended with the accusation that people of a minority sexual orientation might not be welcome. The image was of the hundredth lost sheep which had to be searched for, not only for its own sake but for the sake of the flock as a whole. Majorities can patronise minorities with their concern, but our glimpse took us further than that to the minority as the signpost to salvation for all. Anton Boisen (1968), the founder of the North American pastoral care and counselling movement, believed that under-standing the mentally ill would lead to building 'the city of brotherhood and co-operation on the place where the jungle now stands and greed and ruthless competition rule' (1968: 48). The lost sheep will help the whole flock discover and cherish its lostness.

We begin life as a minority in the hands of a powerful majority. In their respective works, Bowlby (1969) and Winnicott (1971) explore how mutuality of care leads to life and its abundance. 'The good-enough mother starts off with an almost complete adaptation to the infant's needs, and as time proceeds she adapts less and less completely, gradually, according to the infant's growing ability to deal with her failure' (1971: 10). In the last thirty years the liberation theologies have nagged away at the pastoral care and counselling movement, reminding it of the lost. Reit Bonn-Storm (1996) for women, Archie Smith (1982) for black people, Nancy Eiesland (1994) for the disabled, and Stephen

124

Pattison (1994) for those with mental health problems remind us of the movement's neglect of the marginalised.

The minority, the victim, the abused have to speak and have to be heard for the majority's sake as much as for theirs. This is the challenge to pastoral counselling explored in this chapter, through the past and present experience of the modern pastoral counselling movement. What Dorothee Solle (1997) claims theology needs pastoral counselling needs too:

> a right theology needs people in the middle to communicate and ask questions, in other words complaining women, widows and other uneducated people. I don't want to do any more theology without listening to the interlocutors, or being clear about who they are.
>
> (1997: 26–7)

Among the sheep the pastoral movement will always have many interlocutors.

The second theme to emerge from the shadows in Ripon was the *sacred*. This included both the sacred in the holy and religious and the sacred in the therapeutic encounter. We discovered that which we hold most dear, both spiritually and therapeutically, brings us into conflict with each other. The movement is used to this between the different therapeutic models, but religious tensions have been avoided perhaps because we fear their destructiveness. The Ripon conference followed closely upon an international congress in Canada to which other faith groups – Muslim, Native American and Buddhist – were introduced. The promise of pastoral counselling explored in this chapter is to be found wherever fears are faced and differences embraced in faith and practice. In this, we need to forgo authorities we have relied upon. Traditions and beliefs which, like good-enough mothers, have loved us must now begin to fail us.

Looking within the past

Living in the midst of the countryside, watching sheep being sheared, makes the pastoral metaphor familiar in a way that it cannot be in urban societies. However, the BSE crisis is a reminder of the dangers of improper animal husbandry, and the cloning of Dolly brings sheep to the very centre of concern about interference with nature. Although the attachment of *pastoral* to *counselling* can seem anachronistic to many, the pastoral image is still surprisingly revealing of the predicaments and opportunities facing individuals and communities today and especially from a sheep's-eye point of view.

The stories of shepherds and sheep in the Old and New Testaments provide vivid pictures of people's struggle to retain their relationship to God. For the psalmist, 'the Lord is my shepherd, I shall not want' (Psalm 23: 1), and for Ezekiel the Lord himself 'will search for his sheep and will seek them out, as a shepherd seeks out his flock' (Ezekiel 34: 11 and 12). In St John's Gospel (10: 11) Jesus speaks of himself as the good shepherd who lays down his life for the sheep, and in Revelation (7: 17) sheep and shepherd are identified together: 'The lamb who is at the centre of the throne, will be the shepherd, and he will guide them to the springs of life-giving water.'

In the early development of the pastoral care and counselling movement in Britain, Alastair Campbell (1981) rediscovered the significance of the biblical image of the pastor. In the face of counselling's therapeutic seductions he encouraged pastors to welcome the new without letting go of the traditional shepherding of the pastor. 'We can see at once that there is a mixture of tenderness and toughness in the character of the shepherd . . . more like the cowboy of the "Wild West" than the modern shepherd in a settled farming community' (1981: 27). He stresses the shepherd's integrity, courage and willingness to be sacrificed for the flock, in contrast to the clericalising of pastors as leaders in the Church and as counsellors tending to the sufferers. He argues that the pastoral and leadership roles became identified as one and it was 'assumed that *this* leadership is the *only* leadership referred to when we speak of pastoral care. . . . We must learn to speak of the *pastorhood of all believers* and explore the idea that each person has a call to lead in that special way characteristic of the Good Shepherd' (1981: 31, his emphasis). However, it is, I believe, very significant that Campbell assumes that the pastoral image is exclusively about shepherds, and like other authorities (Hiltner 1958; Clinebell 1966; Tidbald 1986; Pattison 1988), he ignores the sheep completely.

It is not difficult to see how the leap is made from God, as shepherd, to God's appointed being shepherds as well. Once the link is made between pastors and leaders, God, as Ezekiel recognised, is always in danger of being displaced:

> As I live, says the Lord God, because my shepherds have not searched out my sheep, but the shepherds have fed themselves, and not fed my sheep, I am against the shepherds. . . . I myself will be the shepherd of my sheep. I will seek the lost, and I will bring back the strayed, and I will bind up the crippled, and

I will strengthen the weak, and the fat and the strong I will watch over; I will feed them justice.

(34: 8–16)

Ezekiel makes it clear that Israel's failed shepherds are their secular not their religious leaders, who have fed themselves and not the people. Contemporary critics of pastoral care and counselling point to the same neglect:

Christian theology needs to ask questions about the politics of therapy and counselling. What are therapy and counselling actually doing about the problems confronting human society?

(Leech 1981: 80)

Are not the counsellors growing fat on their clients' cash if not their food?

Pattison (1988) traces this modern heresy to the unconsidered way in which pastors go about their work, as though pastoral care and counselling is its own justification. 'Such an attitude . . . is indefensible and irresponsible: even, as in the case cited, dangerous' (1998: 1). Clinebell (1966) quotes the parable of life-saving stations established to save ships but grown to look after the interests of the life-savers:

The life saving station became a popular gathering place for its members, and they decorated it beautifully and furnished it exquisitely. Fewer members were now interested in going to sea on life saving missions, so they hired life boat crews to do this work.

(1966: 13)

The parable ends with: 'You will find a number of exclusive clubs along that shore. Shipwrecks are frequent in those waters, but most people drown.' Clinebell then goes on to illustrate, inadvertently, the attractiveness of counselling to counsellors themselves.

The history of pastoral counselling provides evidence of how the pastoral image has been distorted by concentrating upon the shepherd to the exclusion of the sheep. Counselling and psychotherapy reinforce this distortion by replacing theology with the social and human sciences as the basis for training. In 1973, the leaders of the Association for Pastoral Care and Counselling (APCC) produced constitutional papers which describe the movement's fluid and flexible development. At that time, theology and the social and human sciences were equal partners in this.

'Fundamental to the whole enterprise of pastoral work is an understanding of pastoral theology, which takes into account the findings of social sciences' (*Constitutional Papers* 1973: 1). A quarter of a century later their heirs describe the mission and its objectives in the language of contemporary organisational speak:

> The vision of APCC is to encourage, within the British Association for Counselling (BAC) and the faith communities:
> – good practice in pastoral care, and in counselling within the pastoral context.
> – the importance of spirituality as a significant element in the healing, nurture and growth of individuals and communities.
> – the promotion of pastoral care as a distinct and complementary practice to counselling.
>
> (APCC 1998)

Theology is not mentioned and pastoral is only associated with care and not with counselling. In part this is because the Association recognises that in a multi-faith society the word *pastoral* is meaningful only to Christians and Jews. In this climate it is easier for all to find common cause in counselling philosophy and practice than it is to address the many theologies implicit in the different faiths' methods of care. Initially, the word *spiritual* appears to be a good alternative to pastoral. It is recognised by more people as an acceptable way of describing that aspect of human nature which both religion and therapy seek to cherish. It is a word that all faiths understand and that many in secular counselling and care will accept (Thorne 1990). However, the uncritical way in which 'pastoral' is used is a warning against the easy adoption of an even more elusive word (Hay and Nye 1998).

Looking within the remnant

There is evidence to suggest that the word *pastoral* remains as a sign for a remnant. The remnant in biblical tradition are the few who retain their community's vision when the majority are distracted. APCC was originally a gathering of individuals and organisations who struggled to hold on to a vision. They were people from both religious and psychology professions who valued a dialogue that embraced both disciplines, and who found themselves marginalised within their own profession. Holding these worlds together has always been a minority activity and among those who have tried there has always been a tendency for the disciplines of theology and psychology to pull them apart. Wilson (1967), Lambourne (1971) and Pattison (1994) have favoured the theological pole and Clinebell (1966) and Jacobs (1982) the psychological. A less articulate minority have tried, often in vain, to hold to the central ground. Evidence of the remnant's struggle appears in the recurring argument within the editorial committee of the journal *Contact* about the journal being either too academic and theological or too practical and psychological. Within the remnant the word *pastoral* remains consistently if obscurely present as a kind of leaven. Its value as leaven helps disentangle the pastoral metaphor from the distortions occasioned by its identification with shepherds and not sheep. The less it is a patriarchal word the more the fullness of its meaning becomes available. If no one but God is the true Shepherd then the corporateness of the flock and the value of every sheep, especially the hundredth that is lost, gain credibility. This was Lambourne's (1971: 24) vision of pastoral care and counselling as 'lay, corporate, adventurous, variegated and diffuse', truly a pastorhood of all believers.

There are signs that this vision remains a reality among a remnant of those involved in pastoral care and counselling. In this the hidden and within-ness of the *pastoral* is as important to counselling and therapy as it is to spirituality and theology. In all these disciplines things are more than they seem and the *pastoral* in counselling, as in spirituality and theology, represents a special way of recognising the significance of the search for meaning and salvation within human experience – a looking *within*, in contrast to a society which is preoccupied with external reality and looking without. As light on the hill,[2] the *pastoral* in counselling is always open to forms of idolatry, which lead pastors and counsellors into assuming and then being crushed by their omnipotence. The shepherd is not the leader of the community, but the mysterious stranger who, like the angels of Yahweh and the risen Christ, comes and goes, affecting others by his or her presence and absence, rather than by the things done or the status held.

Looking within the present

Whither then is the challenge and promise of pastoral counselling? I think it is to be found not in the activities of a dwindling band of professional pastoral counsellors, impostor shepherds, but hidden among the sheep, diffused in the ministering, caring and counselling activities of many people and institutions, some of which are recognisably religious and others secular and non-religious. Pastoral counselling is not in fact a type of counselling, as Clinebell (1966) called it. It does not have a *core model* beloved of the BAC's courses' accreditation scheme, and it cannot be fitted neatly into the current debate about the differences between psychotherapy, counselling and counselling skills (Foskett and Jacobs 1997). Pastoral counselling is practised using all of the major therapy models and occurs across the whole range of interventions from friendship and care to counselling and psychoanalysis.

There was a debate early in the life of the movement about the use of verbs and nouns. Initially, the verb *counselling* was used and only gradually was this translated into the noun *counsellor*. This continues in the debate about BAC becoming an association for *counsellors* rather than for *counselling*. It is a familiar controversy among those trying to take control of something they value and indeed want to earn their living from, but it is clear that what nouns express statically verbs do dynamically, and counselling is dynamic. Indeed, some of the earliest and most influential research into the effectiveness of counselling and psychotherapy (Truax and Carkhuff 1967) demonstrated that therapists and counsellors who remained engaged in their own development were more effective than colleagues whose development had ceased. So important was this to BAC that impermanence is enshrined in its accreditation procedures. There are parallels in relation to the word *pastoral* becoming *pastor* and then the role of pastor being associated exclusively with professional clergy. Concentrating on the activities rather than the roles is the major challenge and opportunity that can reclaim pastoral counselling from its demise among the clergy and the 'professional' laity.

Pastoral counselling and individuals

In his work with children and patients in psychoanalysis, Donald Winnicott (1971) placed great importance upon what he describes as transitional space and transitional phenomena. By this he means the space between mother and child, mouth and breast which provides all of us with the playground for our beings. Here we begin and begin to become, just as the Hebrew word for God translates as 'I am what I am, I will be what I will be' (Exodus 3: 14). Winnicott uses the word 'breast' to stand for the whole technique of mothering when he writes:

> The breast is created by the infant over and over again out of the infant's capacity to love or (one can say) out of need. A subjective phenomena develops in the baby, which we call the mother's breast. The mother places the actual breast just there where the infant is ready to create, and at the right moment.
>
> (1971: 11)

And to these earliest experiences he traces the roots of culture and spirituality:

> In order to study the play and then the cultural life of the individual one must study the fate of the potential space between any one baby and the human (and therefore fallible) mother figure who is essentially adaptive because of love. . . . For me playing leads naturally to cultural experience and indeed forms its foundation.
>
> (1971: 100–6)

Any activity – care and counselling, friendship and ministry – which draws upon this foundation and allows an individual to uncover their being and their becoming is fulfilling the promise of pastoral counselling for individuals. According to St John in the parable of the good shepherd, Jesus expressed this promise as, 'I came that they might have life and have it abundantly'(10: 10). There is a remarkable example of this in the work of a premature baby unit in Milan. A neuropsychiatrist was invited to contribute to the early diagnosis of cerebral palsy. She began by observing the infants in their incubators and witnessed their intense suffering as they were treated with rectal tubes, bronchial aspiration and the extraction of blood. She noted how parents and staff withdrew to protect themselves from this suffering, attending to the technology rather than the child. Of her observations she writes:

> This experience made me face some primitive and obscure feelings of mine. I felt in a highly violent and painful way how some embryonic mental parts of mine encountered great difficulty in being born psychologically, in finding their right to citizenship.
>
> (Negri 1997: 2)

As she watched, others became more interested in the babies. 'This showed that if somebody was able to think about the baby, all others were stimulated to do so. A circle of thought would begin, that enveloped the baby and included observers, doctors, nurses and parents' (1997: 2).

She discovered that the child who is *thought* about improves physically and the oxygen levels rise in the blood of infants who were *held* in mind although not yet in body. She held meetings with staff around the incubators of the most severely premature babies and led her colleagues in voicing their feelings and observations. 'The nurses have been able to capture and think about vital aspects of the newborn, and as it were "open doors" to the baby inside the incubator' (1997: 2). The same happened for the parents who, when they were helped to observe their infants, began to become mothers and fathers untutored by professional ideas of how parenting should be done.

Although few would call it 'pastoral counselling', most would recognise something akin to it in the group interaction around the incubator. It is harder to make the imaginative jump to see 'pastoral counselling' in the activities of watching and thinking about the infant, until one returns to the image of the good shepherd as the one who knows the sheep by name. 'I noticed . . . that from the third observation the nurse began to approach and comment on the babies' expressiveness' (Negri 1997: 2). And the shepherd who will lay down his or her life for them. 'I felt in a highly violent and painful way how some embryonic mental parts of mine encountered great difficulty in being born' (1997: 2). It is in the watching and the *thinking* about the infants that their lives are 'saved' and the abundance of their personalities anticipated. I am not arguing here that this should be called 'pastoral counselling', rather the opposite; if it were called that it might well cease to have its life-giving properties and become a type of treatment. Better that it remain hidden like leaven.

Pastoral counselling and the community: Church and society

Pastoral counselling is rarely related to communities, let alone society as whole. Its individualistic captivity is all but complete. Major texts on the subject (Clinebell 1966; Jacobs 1982; Estadt 1983; Patton 1990) assume pastoral counselling is conducted between individual counsellors and clients and occasionally with couples and families. Once again, the focus upon the shepherd in his/her professional role rather than upon the sheep (the people) leads to a distortion of the theological metaphor and its rich deposits. The experience of working over many years with groups of people, patients and staff, in psychiatric services convinces me of the more fruitful possibilities of pastoral counselling within communities and whole societies. Counsellors and therapists working within large organisations like colleges and businesses have recognised the same possibilities for their work (Murgatroyd 1993). A remnant among therapists has retained this knowledge (Menzies-Lyth 1988) and demonstrated that the fruit of the shepherding that emerges from within the flock is not identified with the skill of the pastor or the therapist.

In *Christianity Rediscovered* (1978), Vincent Donovan records his work among the Masai people of East Africa. He found a way of meeting with a community of Masai through an exchange of stories:

> I soon realised that not one week would go by without some surprising rejoinder or reaction or revelation from the Masai. . . . I was more than startled when a young Masai elder stood up and said 'If ever I run into God, I will put a spear through him.' He was immersed on one side in an unshakable belief in the existence of God, and faced on the other with the numbing reality of a life that includes pain and sickness, death of children and loss of cattle. This young elder was trying to come to terms with a God who seemed to be responsible for it all.
>
> (1978: 412)

This conversation prompted more reflection about Engai, the Masai God, and about the Christian God. The Masai have many names for God, male and female. And they were surprised to learn that 'we (Christians) leave the female out of God' (Donovan 1978: 42). On this occasion the discussion developed around the location for God. Engai does not leave the Masai territory and the idea of a universal God was alien to them. Donovan told them about the Jewish God who had become enslaved to a country and a people and how, when Abraham led them out of that country, God was free to be universal. He suggested that perhaps Engai had become trapped in the Masai's country, and they needed to follow him like Abraham to find the High God of all tribes, who loves all people. One listener asked, 'This story of Abraham – does it speak only to the Masai? Or does it speak also to you? Has your tribe found the High God? Have you known him?' (1978: 45). Donovan had to contemplate the way in which Western denominations and societies laid claim to the Christian God as being theirs, so he was surprised to hear himself say, 'No, we have not found the High God. My tribe has not known him. For us too he is the unknown God. . . . Let us search for him together. Maybe together we will find him' (1978: 46).

   The work done by the analytic *remnant* associated with the Tavistock Institute of Human Relations has done much to reveal the significance of 'pastoral counselling' in a secular form within institutions and society as a whole. The work was begun after the Second World War when Wilfred Bion (1961) attempted to learn what the 'lost', those psychologically traumatised by war, had to teach about the unconscious processes within groups and communities. This work became more explicitly pastoral when the focus was turned upon religious groups and communities and their roles within society as a whole (Reed 1978; Miller 1993; Lawrence 1995). A recent example comes from a lecture given by Gordon Lawrence to hospital chaplains, whose work often involves them in pastoral counselling with individuals. Because chaplains 'symbolise the transcendent and the possibility of a relatedness between humans and the divine, they become privy to what cannot be voiced in the Health System . . . they become one of the rare places within the system where existential preoccupations can be lodged' (Lawrence 1995: 20). Just as the pastoral counsellor with individuals works to bring into thought an individual's known but unspoken anxieties, Lawrence suggests that chaplains may do the same for their institutions. Once the unthought knowns are thought and voiced, 'it makes a difference because this new information, which was always known, if only unconsciously or subliminally, now becomes part of the acknowledged, spoken culture' (1995: 21). In hospital, it is likely that the 'unthought knowns' are about tragedy and death and, of course, it is to these events that chaplains are summoned urgently. Because chaplains are alert to individual tragedies they are also aware of the unthinkable and unspeakable tragedies of whole institutions and of the society for which those institutions care, as in Westminster Abbey's response to the death of Princess Diana. Chaplains, like Donovan and the Masai elders, are the access points to people's engagement with the tragic and existential realities of life, and their theologies, fashioned in response to previous tragedies, are a rich resource for their shepherding.

Gordon Lawrence and Eric Miller (1993) defined the primary task of ministry for an Anglican diocese as:

> to illuminate the interrelatedness of the teachings of the Church with contemporary experience of members of society. . . . To be effective it must at once be looking back into the teachings of Christ and the Bible and into the traditions of the Church, and outwards into the problems and preoccupations of contemporary society.
>
> (Miller 1993: 107–8)

In practice, this might occur in the following way. A mental health service manager comes to supervision with her supervisor, who is practising pastoral supervision (Foskett and Lyall 1988). She tells him of an arson attack by a client in her clinic that terrified everyone. He explores with her how her institution has failed her in not providing the security measures she wanted. She expresses her own failure in not insisting upon them. He encourages her to be more assertive and hears that she plans to enlist the clients to bring pressure to bear upon her managers. In the whole of her supervision, no mention is made of the client who set the fire and what his action means. It is left to the supervisor's consultant to draw attention to this.

What is the anxiety/frustration which led a client to express their unthought known in such a dangerous way and what led everyone to ignore that act and become embroiled in a battle about physical safety? For the pastoral counsellor, the answers to these questions are likely to emerge when the unthought knowns are brought into thought and then expression, where they can contribute to the task of the unit in caring for and treating its clients. For instance, a meeting of all clients, staff and managers to discuss what happened and what people thought and felt would probably reveal many unexpressed fears and hopes for everyone to explore. If the client who set the fire could also express his thoughts and feelings, the ninety and nine would have the benefit of the lost hundredth's point of view as well. Then, the whole flock would be shepherding and counselling one another and the pastorhood of all believers could be a reality.

Pastoral counselling and the many faiths

The roots of pastoral care and pastoral counselling are in the Judaeo-Christian tradition but their growth has blossomed in psychological rather than religious, social, theological or political soil (Lambourne 1971; Oden 1984; Pattison 1988, 1994). Some pastors and counsellors want to broaden that base in two ways: first, to engage more directly with religious, social, theological and political critiques of pastoral counselling; and second, to be open to other faith groups and to those who value non-religious spirituality (Hay and Nye 1998), in order to draw upon the resources of other cultures and contexts as well as Christian and Jewish. The APCC has worked hard to create an environment in which Western pastoral care and counselling would not dominate inter-faith and inter-cultural exploration.

Emmanuel Lartey (1997) has contributed much to these developments, knowing as he does both West African and European contexts. For him, a return to theology provides a way forward.

> Pastoral care ... requires a broad and deep engagement with living persons in their universal, cultural and unique character-istics. It seeks to pay careful attention to the impact of each one of these three influences on every person. ... Intercultural

pastoral care has to be a corporate, cooperative activity in
which *many* work together for *each* and for *all*.

(1997: 125, his emphasis)

He offers pastoral counsellors a fruitful combination of theology and
therapy that reflects the theme of hiddenness explored above:

Pastoral care needs to go through a process of *kenosis*. By
kenosis is meant an emptying of selfhood. In Christian understanding Christ's 'emptying' of himself in the incarnation is the
heart of the gospel. *Kenosis* . . . is the characteristic of the life
of the God who is constantly engaging in acts of self giving.
. . . It is my view that the time has come for the essence of
'pastoral care' to be freed from the captivity of its 'self hood' in
terms of its origins, in order to engage in real terms with the
pluralism of the current world. Will it by doing so lose its
essence and identity? I think not, for it is in such self-emptying
that its true being-in-the-world may be realised.

(1997: 133)

Lartey, like Vanstone (1977), goes on to explore the incarnate nature
of this kenosis, which encourages a curiosity and openness to the truth
about humanity and divinity present in all cultures and traditions, thus
inviting us to go with Donovan and the Masai in searching together for
the High God, who loves all people.

Theology is going through a similar experience of self-emptying.
In the short essays of the leading European theologians (Moltmann
1997) there are many references to this. 'Only at a late stage did I come
to realise how remote our prevailing christological and theological
abstractions made us from real possibilities of realization, from real
action and from the trust of Jesus in his brothers and sisters' (1997: 27).
None is more poignant than Johann Metz. As a mere sixteen-year-old he
wandered through burning villages to find his company:

I found only the dead: dead bodies. . . . I could only look into
still faces of all those with whom the previous days I had shared
my anxieties of childhood and the joys of youth, I can not
remember anything but a silent cry. I can still see myself there
today, and my childhood dreams collapsed before that memory.
A great gap had been torn in my powerful Bavarian catholic
socialisation with its well-knit trust.

(Moltmann 1997: 32)

Thus emptied of his beliefs he, like other German theologians, was forced to confront the chasm in which he found 'those who speak of God as Jesus does, take into account the possibility of the destruction of their own preconceived certainties by the misfortune of others' (1997: 33).

In his theology of the Old Testament Walter Breuggeman (1997) identifies the same kenotic formula within his discipline. 'The practical manifestation of this must be honoured in a multi layered pluralism that is newly insistent in the discipline of Old Testament studies' (1997: xv). He identifies three kinds of pluralism: a pluralism of faith affirmations, of methods and of interpretive communities. The received traditions both of text and of scholarship can be reverenced and relied upon no longer. They must be examined from whence they have come, for what in that context shaped them, and for the effect consequent faith and scholarship have had upon them. The testimony of Israel can no more be seen as *the dominant meta-narrative* for Christians and Jews, let alone for everyone else. Now, there are no meta-narratives to bring order out of chaos. All are equally available as 'subversive protests and as alternative visions, which invite criticism and transformation' (1997: 713).

Breuggeman goes on to argue that our postmodern world frees us to see the pluralism hidden within the scriptures themselves. Wherever one looks 'from the ground up the texts witness to plurality of testimonies concerning God and Israel's life with God' (Breuggeman 1997: 710). He gives examples of the different responses to the Exile and the truth they reveal about Yahweh and of the decision to hold both priestly and Deuteronomic traditions in tension. The texts manifest dispute and compromise and treat all conclusions as provisional:

> Because different interpretations in different contexts – driven by different hopes, fears, and hurts – ask different questions from the ground up, it is clear that there will be no widely accepted 'Canon within the Canon'. . . . As a consequence we are now able to see that every interpretation is context driven and interest driven to some large extent.
>
> (1997: 711)

The process of self-emptying has to engage us all and for once theology is helping us grasp the fact that this has always been the real story whatever establishments have told us.

Pastoral counselling: looking to the future

So it is the followers, the sheep and not the shepherds, who are central to any understanding of the pastoral metaphor. What is the perspective from the ground up and from a sheep's-eye view? All faith groups and those with spiritual concerns know instinctively the authority that speaks from the bottom of experience. Victim speaking to victim is 'the most permanent therapy for societies as well as individuals' (Urban 1996: 7). All the therapeutic traditions have valued this knowledge above all other, but in practice they conform to society's belief in the importance of the shepherds rather than sheep. Counsellors', analysts' and psychotherapists' own treatment precedes any work they do for others and their practice continually returns them to the scrutiny of their own psyches. And yet the temptations of knowledge and the vanity of wisdom seduce them too. Counselling is much absorbed with earning credibility, and pastors are not far behind in wanting worldly acknowledgement (BAC and APCC strategic plans 1998–2003). And so the emptying of self, of institutions and orthodoxies so urgently recognised by some in theology and pastoral care and counselling will not be welcomed by religious or therapeutic establishments whose mission statements, unquestioned doctrines and manic activity hold them in thrall. This is the challenge to pastoral counselling.

In *Playing and Reality*, Winnicott (1971) expounds the value of what he calls 'transitional space and phenomena'; that is, the space and objects, initially between mother (breast) and infant, in which and by which we become ourselves. Here, religion and culture are born and take shape. Different societies and cultures respect and nurture this space and place in different ways. In Western society, counselling, psychoanalysis and psychotherapy have provided one medium for this. Winnicott writes of how he came lately to recognise that what and how he was in the analytic space mattered more than anything he did or said. In fact, he had to be emptied and to sacrifice what he would do and say for the sake of his patients:

> It appals me to think how much deep change I have prevented or delayed in patients . . . by my personal need to interpret. If only we can wait, the patient arrives at understanding creatively and with immense joy, and I now enjoy this joy more than I used to enjoy the sense of being clever. I think I interpret mainly to let the patient know the limits of my understanding. The principle is that it is the patient and only the patient who has the answers.
>
> (1971: 86)

The promise of pastoral counselling is to *enjoy* that *joy*. How would it be to make interpretations, statements, testimonies, or doctrines in order to let others know not our wisdom but the limits of our knowledge? Not in order to convert all to one point of view, but to empty ourselves of where we are in order to make room for where we will be. Is this not after all the Christian experience of a self-emptying, becoming God? 'With the collapse of metaphysics comes the loss of the self-evident God, who looks remarkably like the un-self-evident God of the biblical stories. The God who is not the answer to all human questions but the question to all human answers' (Teilman 1996: 13). We become whatever religion or non-religion we are in order to become human and not vice versa, and by implication any faith or non-faith tradition has no place to follow or judge any other except in the search for its humanity. In this, the challenge and promise of pastoral counselling find common ground.

NOTES

1 The European Association for Pastoral Care and Counselling has held conferences every four years since 1972. I am indebted to Hermann Steinkamp, whose paper 'Foreigners – richness and threat' helped illuminate the *marginalised* theme in Ripon, and to Barbara Schneider and Mark Sutherland whose contributions helped me identify the *sacred* theme.
2 Matthew 5: 16 'Let your light so shine before men that they may see your good works' contrasted with Matthew 13:33 'The Kingdom of Heaven is like leaven, which a woman took and hid in three measures of meal, till it was all leavened.'

REFERENCES

APCC (1973) *Constitutional Papers*, APCC, Rugby: Association for Pastoral Care and Counselling.
APCC (1998) *Mission and Objectives*, APCC, Rugby: Association for Pastoral Care and Counselling.
BAC (1998) *Strategic Plan*, BAC, Rugby: British Association for Counselling.
Bion, W. (1961) *Experiences in Groups*, London: Tavistock.
Boisen, A. (1968) *American Journal of Pastoral Psychology*, 22(3): 48.
Bonn-Storm, R. (1996) *The Incredible Woman: Listening to Women's Silences in Pastoral Care and Counselling*, Nashville: Abingdon.
Bowlby, J. (1969) *Attachment and Loss*, London: Hogarth.
Breuggeman, W. (1997) *Theology of the Old Testament*, Nashville: Abingdon.
Campbell, A. (1981) *Rediscovering Pastoral Care*, London: Darton, Longman & Todd.

Clinebell, H. (1966) *Basic Types of Pastoral Counselling*, Nashville: Abingdon.

Donovan, V. (1978) *Christianity Rediscovered*, London: SCM.

Eiesland, N. (1994) *The Disabled God*, Nashville: Abingdon.

Estadt, B. (1983) *Pastoral Counselling*, Englewood Cliffs, NJ: Prentice Hall.

Foskett, J. and Jacobs, M. (1997) 'Pastoral counselling', in S. Palmer (ed.), *Handbook of Counselling*, London, Routledge, 317–31.

Foskett, J. and Lyall, D. (1988) *Helping the Helpers: Pastoral Supervision*, London: SPCK.

Hay, D. and Nye, R. (1998) *The Spirit of the Child*, London: Fount.

Hiltner, S. (1958) *Preface to Pastoral Theology*, New York: Abingdon.

Jacobs, M. (1982) *Still Small Voice*, London: SPCK.

Lambourne, R. (1971) 'Objections to a national pastoral organisation', *Contact*, 35: 24–9.

Lartey, E. (1997) *In Living Colour*, London: Cassell.

Lawrence, G. (1995) 'The seductiveness of totalitarian states-of-mind', *Journal of Health Care Chaplaincy*, October: 11–22.

Leech, K. (1981) *The Social God*, London: Sheldon.

Menzies-Lyth, I. (1988) *Containing Anxiety in Institutions: Selected Essays*, vol. 1, London: Free Association Books.

Miller, E. (1993) *From Dependency to Autonomy*, London: Free Association Books.

Moltmann, J. (ed.) (1997) *How I have Changed*, London: SCM.

Murgatroyd, S. (1993) 'Symposium: Counselling and the Organisation', *British Journal of Guidance and Counselling*, 21: 2.

Negri, R. (1997) 'The newborn in the Department of Neonatal Intensive Care Unit (NICU): a neuropsychological model of prevention', University of Milan (unpublished paper).

Oden, T. (1984) *Care of Souls in the Classic Tradition*, Philadelphia: Fortress.

Pattison, S. (1988) *A Critique of Pastoral Care*, London: SCM.

—— (1994) *Pastoral Care and Liberation Theology*, Cambridge: Cambridge University Press.

Patton, J. (1990) 'Pastoral counselling', in R. Hunter (ed.), *Dictionary of Pastoral Care and Counseling*, Nashville: Abingdon, 849–54.

Reed, B. (1978) *The Dynamics of Religion*, London: Darton, Longman & Todd.

Smith, A. (1982) *The Relational Self: Ethics and Therapy from a Black Perspective*, Nashville: Abingdon.

Solle, D. (1997) in J. Moltmann (ed.), *How I have Changed*, London: SCM, 22–8.

Teilman, D. (1996) 'Changing belief in a changing culture', *Contact*, 119: 12–14.

Thorne, B. (1990) 'Symposium: Spiritual Dimensions in Counselling', *British Journal of Guidance and Counselling*, 18: 3.

Tidbald, D. (1986) *Skilful Shepherd*, Leicester: Apollos.

Truax, C. B. and Carkhuff, R. R. (1967) *Towards Effective Counselling and Psychotherapy*, Chicago: Aldine.

Urban, J. (1996) 'Everything is breaking down: can you help me?' *Contact*, 119: 5–6.

Vanstone, W. (1977) *Love's Endeavour Love's Expense*, London: Darton, Longman & Todd.

Wilson, M. (1967) *The Church is Healing*, London: SCM.

Winnicott, D. (1971) *Playing and Reality*, London: Routledge.

INDEX